A MONTH-BY-MONTH GUIDE

TIME OUT

TO ACTIVITIES TO ENJOY

TOGETHER

WITH YOUR CHILDREN

Jan Brennan

August House / Little Rock
PUBLISHERS

© Copyright 1990 by Jan Brennan
All rights reserved. This book, or parts thereof,
may not be reproduced in any form without permission.
Published by August House, Inc.,
P.O. Box 3223, Little Rock, Arkansas, 72203,
501-372-5450.

Printed in the United States of America

10 9 8 7 6 5 4 3 2

LIBRARY OF CONGRESS CATALOGING-IN-PUBLICATION DATA

Brennan, Jan, 1952–
Time out together / Jan Brennan. — 1st ed.
p.   cm.
ISBN 0-87483-103-2 (alk. paper) : $12.95
1. Family recreation—United States. 2. Creative activities and
seat work.   I. Title.
GV182.8.B74   1990
649'.5—dc20
                                                          89-27354
                                                          CIP

Design and production by Designed Communications
Typography by Lettergraphics, Memphis, Tennessee
Project direction by Hope Coulter

This book is printed on archival-quality paper which meets the
guidelines for performance and durability of the Committee on
Production Guidelines for Book Longevity of the Council on
Library Resources.

AUGUST HOUSE, INC.   PUBLISHERS   LITTLE ROCK

To Lee, my best critic, my best support, and my best friend, and to Michael, Matthew, and Kyle, my three inspirations with whom I love to take "time out together"

CONTENTS

ACKNOWLEDGMENTS

I wish to thank Susan Knopf, for her professional assistance; Nancy DeSalvo, Peter Guglietta, and Gail Ryan, three very helpful librarians, for their time and aid; Ray and Agnes Cuatto, my parents, for their continuing support and love; Sandy Cuatto and Lis Cristafaro for their legal advice; and the rest of my family and my dear friends for their enthusiasm and support.

INTRODUCTION

We live in a very busy time. Adults and children alike face many demands in their over-scheduled lives. It may seem that there are too few hours in the day to accomplish all we wish to do.

If you were to make a list of what you wanted to do tomorrow, what would be on it? Would reading and playing with your child be there? Spending quality time with the children we love is important for both us and them. Each time an experience is shared, the bond between the two parties grows stronger. We owe it to our children as well as to ourselves to find some quality time to enjoy each other's company.

This book can't help you find that time. But it will help give you ideas of fun things to do with your child when you do take time out together.

The book is organized in the following fashion: There are twelve chapters, one for each month of the year. Each chapter is further divided into four or five sections—fifty-two in all. Each of these sections focuses on a particular theme, with related books, poems, songs, recipes, art projects, and activities that follow. You may do one activity each day, following this as a daily guide, or you may decide to pick and choose activities in a more random, individual fashion. Do whatever fits most comfortably and naturally with your particular schedule. The way you use this book is not important; the key is that you and your child enjoy each other and take some quality time out together.

CHAPTER ONE

JANUARY
A Month of Snow Days

January, for many people, is a month filled with snow. One snowstorm is barely over before the next one begins. But January isn't synonymous with snow everywhere. Some parts of the world never have snow at all. Just think—while children are snow-skiing in one part of the world, others somewhere else may be water-skiing! While some children are sipping hot chocolate to warm frosty toes, others may be sipping frosty lemonade to cool steamy toes.

Whether you live where January snow is a reality or just a dream, the activities in this chapter offer snow play ideas that you can adapt to your own weather. While some of you may go outside to make snow angels, others might make "sand" angels. Real snow or pretend—make this January one that is filled with snow fun every day.

FIRST WEEK

Attention: Missing Mittens

Mittens are hard to find when you need them. You've probably tried to clip them onto the wristbands of coats; perhaps you've connected them to each other with yarn and threaded them through jackets; you might even have bought five pairs and placed them in strategic locations. But I bet you still hear this familiar declaration: "I can't find my mittens!" So you search every nook and cranny of the house, weed through every coat pocket, poke around under the car seats, cross-examine the cat and dog, and finally succumb to bringing out that last "emergency-only" pair. Don't let lost mittens get the best of you. This chapter's activities will help you see mittens in a different light.

READINGS

The Mystery of the Missing Red Mitten by Steven Kellogg (Dial Books for Young Readers)

Annie is thoroughly enjoying herself playing in the snow until she realizes she has lost her fifth mitten of the winter. Her amusing find sheds new light on lost mittens.

The Mitten by Alvin Tresselt (Lothrop; pb Scholastic)

While gathering firewood for his grandmother on the coldest day of the winter, a little boy drops one of his mittens. Within minutes it becomes a haven for some very interesting visitors.

One-Mitten Lewis by Helen Kay (Lothrop, Lee & Shepard Co.)

Lewis has a mitten problem—he always seems to lose one mitten of every pair he owns. Not only is Lewis frustrated, but so is his mother, until they arrive at a novel solution to this universal problem.

RECITINGS

WARM AND SNUG
(Sung to "Where Is Thumbkin?")

Where is Thumbkin, where is Thumbkin?
Here I am, here I am.
Hiding in this mitten,
Warm as my pet kitten,
Warm and snug, warm and snug.

Where is Pointer, ***etc.***

Where is Tall Man, ***etc.***

Where is Ring Man, ***etc.***

Where is Pinkie, ***etc.***

Where are all the men, ***etc.***

WINTER DRESS-UP
(Sung to "Ten Little Indians")

One little, two little, three pairs of stockings,
Four little, five little, six pairs of leggings,
Seven little, eight little, nine shirts for tucking,
Ten layers underneath.

Next come the snow pants,
Next comes the jacket,
A boot for each foot
If I can latch it;
Mittens, scarf, and hat,
All to match it—
I'm ready to play outside.

But now that I'm ready, I have one problem—
I can't seem to stand up from my bottom.
All these layers—I'm glad I've got 'em,
But it's oh so hard to move!

A BRIEF NOTE ABOUT THE RECIPES IN THIS BOOK

Cooking with children can be very rewarding for both adult and child. It not only allows an opportunity for great learning to take place, but also provides for the sharing of some quality time. The extent to which you encourage your child to participate, however, is entirely up to you. One parent may want his child right by his side, elbow-deep in the preparations, while another may limit the involvement to getting out the ingredients. Only you know your patience and your child's abilities. Therefore, the recipes have been written with the instructions directed to the adult. Please incorporate your child into the recipes as much and as often as you're comfortable with doing.

RECIPES

MITTEN MIX

Here is a high-energy snack to stuff in your mittens and take with you on winter outings.

Mix in a bowl equal portions of raisins, peanuts, sunflower seeds, carob chips, cashews. Add any other nuts or seeds you like, or substitute for those listed. Divide up into small plastic bags and put a twist tie around each bag.

When ready for an outing hold one bag in the palm of your hand, then slip on your mitten. You'll have a snack all ready for munching.

INSTANT COCOA

The advantage of making your own instant chocolate mix is that you can control how much cocoa and sugar are used.

1. Mix 1 cup dry milk powder, 2 tablespoons cocoa, and 1 teaspoon sugar. Sift three times and store, tightly covered, in the refrigerator.
2. To serve, place 3 to 4 heaping teaspoons of the mixture in a cup. Stir in hot milk or hot water.

ACTIVITIES

HOMEMADE MITTENS

This activity is a follow-up to *The Mitten* by Alvin Tresselt.

Trace your child's hand (fingers together in a mitten style) on a double thickness of construction paper. (Make it a little larger than actual hand size). Cut it out. You will have two identical cutouts.

Using a paper punch, punch holes about every half-inch around the outside border of the cut-outs except the wrist opening.

Help your child "sew" the two pieces of mitten together by lacing through the holes with yarn. Be sure to leave an opening for the hand at the wrist.

Tie a knot at each end.

Decorate the mitten if desired, using crayons, markers, sequins, feathers, and cotton balls.

MITTEN GAMES

Dramatize *The Mitten* by having your child stuff the mitten she made in the activity above with various items that can represent the animals in the book, such as cutout pictures or plastic figures, or choose something else she wants. The fun begins when she continues to stuff until the mitten "explodes" apart, leaving everything strewn all over.

HIDE-AND-SEEK MITTEN SEARCH

This game can be played indoors or outdoors.

Use one brightly-colored mitten. Designate a hiding vicinity (for example, only in the back yard around the swing set). Take turns being the hider and the seeker of the mitten.

JANUARY GAMES

OUTDOOR TRACKING

As soon as there is enough snow on the ground to allow footprints to show, take a nature walk through some woods, having your child pay close attention to animal tracks. See if he can find any tracks of mice, squirrels, cats, dogs, rabbits, and birds. If there are not good tracks on your own property, perhaps a short ride to a nearby park would be worthwhile. On city sidewalks, he can compare the dog tracks—little dogs, big dogs, running dogs, and digging dogs. If there is no snow, try looking for tracks on sandy beaches, dirt roads, or muddy paths.

ADD-ON

This great memory game is fun and challenging and requires good listening skills and concentration.

Begin by saying, "I was trudging through the forest gathering firewood for my grandmother when I saw . . ." Then fill in the blank.

The first person names one thing, for example, a mouse.

The next person says, "I was trudging through the forest gathering firewood for my grandmother when I saw a mouse and . . ."—and adds one more thing, let's say a rabbit.

The game continues with each turn adding one more item to the list.

SECOND WEEK

Snow Day Play

Snow is falling, roads are closed, all plans for the day have been canceled. Today is a bonus day—a day off with nothing specific to do. So don your snow gear and head for the outdoors. There is plenty of snow-play waiting for you just outside your front door.

Before you and your little one bundle up in all your layers of warmth, cuddle up and read some of the snowy books listed below, to create the right atmosphere.

READINGS

The Snowy Day by Ezra Jack Keats (Viking; pb Penguin)

When Peter wakes up one winter morning to find his world blanketed in white snow, he can't wait to get outside to play in it. Ezra Jack Keats vividly describes and illustrates Peter's activities.

Anna's Snow Day by Louise Gunther (Garrard)

School is canceled due to a big snowstorm and Anna couldn't be happier. She and her friend, Rose, have a sparkling day as they find all kinds of fun things to do in the city.

First Snow by Emily Arnold McCully (Harper & Row Junior Books)

Little Mouse is not quite so brave as his seven siblings when they all take to the hills to go sledding. This wordless picture book will delight all who have ever looked timidly at a steep snow-covered hill.

A BRIEF NOTE ABOUT WORDLESS PICTURE BOOKS

Wordless picture books are wonderful books for prereaders, for they allow the child to "read" the story through interpreting the pictures, using her own experience and her own words. This supplies a powerful and proud feeling of accomplishment for a child.

RECITINGS

SNOWFLAKES FALLING
(sung to "Frère Jacques")

Snowflakes falling, snowflakes falling,
All around, all around—
Snowflakes on the trees
And snowflakes on the greens,
And on the ground, on the ground.

Snowflakes falling, snowflakes falling,
Wherever I go, wherever I go—
Snowflakes in the air
And snowflakes in my hair—
I love them so, I love them so.

SNOW, SNOW
(Sung to "Rain, Rain")

Snow, snow, came last night,
Soft, white snow, such a delight,
I can't wait to play outside,
Get on my sled, go for a ride.

Snow, snow, treasures white,
Bringing fun and lovely sights,
Footprints, angels, snowball fun,
I hope this snow is never gone.

RECIPES

SNOWBALLS

Using a melon baller, scoop out balls of ice cream (vanilla for correct coloring, but really any flavor will do).

Roll the balls in coconut.

Refreeze or serve immediately.

With snowballs this size, you can serve more than one per person. Perhaps your child can make a snowball wall, a snowman, a snow fort . . . let your imaginations run wild.

SNOWCONES

Using an ice crusher, or by placing ice cubes in a plastic bag and banging with a wooden spoon, crush several ice cubes. Put the well-crushed ice in a paper cup. Pour 2 to 3 tablespoons of your favorite juice over it.

SNOWFLAKE LUNCH BOX

Peanut butter and snowflake sandwiches: sprinkle coconut on peanut butter as your snow.

Chicken snowflake soup: chicken rice soup with a dash of imagination to turn the rice into snowflakes.

Snowflake milk: coconut sprinkled in milk.

For dessert, serve either Snowballs or Snowcones.

Try using unsweetened coconut available in health food stores. No one will miss the sugar.

ACTIVITIES

OUTDOOR PLAY

Parallel Peter's activities in **The Snowy Day** with your child by:

■ making footprints in the snow in various patterns (this is fun in damp sand, too);

■ using a stick to make tracks or drawings in snow, mud, or sand;

■ using a stick to smack snow off branches of trees (or raindrops after a heavy rainfall);

■ making snow angels, sand angels, or leaf angels after autumn leaves have fallen;

■ being a mountain climber—climb a hill of snow, then slide down.

Of course, there is always sledding fun, where even the smallest of hills is a thrill. If you have no hills on your property, attach a rope to the sled and pull your child for a special ride (and a great aerobic workout for you). If you have no snow, a wagon and a vivid imagination will do!

For an eternal childhood favorite: just before coming inside let your child make a snowball or two to put in the freezer to save for a hot summer day. (Put the snowball in a freezer bag to preserve its shape over time.)

MAKE-A-FLAKE

Paper Snowflakes: Give your child white paper. Have her fold the paper in half two times, then cut out tiny little shapes (circles, triangles, ovals) from the edges. Unfold.

For younger children, have your child decorate the paper before you cut it out as a snowflake. Or use a really big piece of paper and draw lines on it to guide your child's cutting.

With your finished snowflakes, make a mobile by using thread to hang them from a hanger, or tape them to windows; the light will shine through for a special effect.

Yarn Snowflakes: Use a 3-by-5-inch index card as a spindle and have your child wrap white yarn around the width of the card, making several layers to cover the card completely. Help her to slip the yarn carefully off the card. While she holds the bundled yarn, you can tie it snugly in the middle with another piece of yarn. With scissors, cut through the loops at the top and bottom of the yarn bundle. Fluff ends to make a round, puffy snowflake.

Then use these snowflakes as a ball for catching games, one attached to either end of a paper towel tube as a baton for relay races, or as festive decorations. To dress up your yarn snowflakes, glue on sequins and small pieces of colored ribbons.

THIRD WEEK

Snowplows Are for Kids, Too

To a child, driving a powerful snowplow through drifting snowbanks and snowy roads seems like nothing but sheer fun and excitement. This chapter's activities can be grouped into two categories: map-making and snowplowing. Before snowplow operators can start work, they must have a map of the area to be plowed. Therefore, before you and your child plunge into your pretend plowing activities, sit down and have fun drawing up some maps. The following suggestions will help you do both.

READINGS

Katy and the Big Snow by Virginia Lee Burton (Houghton Mifflin Co.)

The City of Geoppolis is covered with more than five feet of snow. Everyone and everything is stopped until Katy, the most powerful snowplow owned by the Geoppolis Highway Department, goes to work. Can Katy singlehandedly plow out the entire town?

The Day Daddy Stayed Home by Ethel and Leonard Kessler (pb Doubleday & Co.)

It's the biggest snow of the year and Daddy has to

stay home because the streets aren't plowed. This book shows some of the excitement a young boy and his dad have on their snow day together.

The Big Snow by Berta and Elmer Hader (Macmillan)

What does a big snowfall mean to the many woodland animals? This gentle story about the preparations and various accommodations made by animals in winter answers that question beautifully.

RECITINGS

Snowplows
(Sung to "I'm a Little Teapot")

I'm a great big snowplow
Strong and tough,
When it comes to work
I never get enough.
When the snow gets real deep
Hear me puff,
"How I love to plow that cold white stuff!"

Plowing with My Snowplow
(Sung to "Working on the Railroad")

I've been plowing with my snowplow
All the livelong day,
I've been plowing with my snowplow,
Just to push the snow away;
Don't you hear my snowplow scraping,
Scraping the snow away?
Can't you see the roads a-clearing?
I'm doing my job today.

Out to clear the roads,
Out to clear the snows,
Out to clear the roads today—
Out to clear the roads,
Out to clear the snows,
Plowing with my plow today.

RECIPES

PLOWED GOULASH
Your child can even plow right through his dinner.

1. Mix together in a large frying pan 2 cups cooked hamburger meat or cooked ground turkey; 2 cups cooked rice; 2 cups cooked vegetable of your choice; and 2 cups spaghetti sauce.
2. Heat through and add salt and pepper to taste. Dish out enough on each plate to make a thin covering over the entire plate, using a small plate if your child has a small appetite. Show your child how the fork can be used as a snowplow and proceed to plow the streets clean. Parmesan cheese may be sprinkled over the goulash as added "snow."

SNOW PUDDING
Again, cover the entire plate and instruct your young snowplow operator to use a spoon to begin cleaning up the streets. For extra fun use pineapple chunks or other pieces of fruit or dried fruit to represent houses and buildings.

1. Combine $\frac{1}{3}$ cup sugar, 2 tablespoons cornstarch, and $\frac{1}{8}$ teaspoon salt in a 2-quart pan.
2. Blend 2 cups milk and 2 egg yolks, slightly beaten, in a bowl.
3. Gradually stir milk mixture into sugar mixture, then put pan on stove.
4. Cook over medium heat, stirring constantly, until thick and bubbly; boil gently one minute, stirring, then remove from heat and continue stirring for a few minutes.
5. Stir in 2 teaspoons vanilla.
6. Pour into dishes; cool. To serve, pour cooled pudding out onto a plate for plowing.
   Makes 4 servings.

There are many other foods that you can use to plow. Brainstorm with your child and see how many other snowplow meals you can come up with.

ACTIVITIES

MAP-MAKING

Make a simple map using pencils, paper, and crayons.

Choose one of the following to map with your child:

■ Your house: First you should draw the floor plan, then allow your child to add the furnishings (it's interesting to see what the most important furnishings are in each room in your child's eye).

■ Your neighborhood: Draw your street and plot where your house is. Then allow your child to add the neighbors' houses.

■ Your town: Begin with your house on your street, then continue to draw in the main roads that lead you to frequently visited places. Work with your child to locate such places as friends' houses, nursery school, library, stores, restaurants. This will require a large piece of paper. Brown wrapping paper or the unwaxed side of freezer paper works well for a larger map.

FLOOR MAP

Use masking tape to lay out one of the maps you and your child drew in the map-making activity. Use toy furniture, toys, cutouts from magazines, and homemade signs or pictures to furnish or label your floor map. For example, if you want to map your town, let masking tape be its roads. Make as many roads from your house as you and your child have the time and energy for. Let toy houses and buildings represent buildings such as your house, your neighbors' houses, the doctor's office, the grocery store, and the gas station. Label them by writing with a permanent marker on the masking tape. When the floor map is finished, take turns "walking" various routes. (Masking tape left on the floor for an extended time may leave a residue, so you may not wish to leave your floor map down for more than a day. Or try this activity outside, on a plowed drive.)

INDOOR SNOWPLOWING

If the weather is not cooperating, here is a recipe to make indoor snow-sand to plow.

Mix equal portions of cornmeal and raw rice, or 2 cups dried used coffee grounds, $1/2$ cup flour, 1 cup cornmeal, and $1/4$ cup salt.

Put the mixture in an old baby bathtub or a large dishpan.

Supply various small toys and plastic containers for your child's play in the snow-sand. Also try plowing your map route, or plowing a pretend route like the one Katy plowed in *Katy and the Big Snow.* (Depending on your child's dexterity, you may wish to put a large sheet down under the dishpan of snow-sand to avoid a messy clean-up.)

FOURTH WEEK

Snowman Fantasy

A snowstorm without a snowman is like a snow-covered hill without children sledding. Snowmen are important and exciting parts of children's snow play. But what makes them so intriguing? What leads children repeatedly to create snowman after snowman? Is it an artistic desire to be creative with this freshly-made natural medium? Could it simply be the fun of the invigorating physical activity involved? Or might it be a subconscious hope that maybe, just maybe, this snowman might possess some magical powers and become real? Share some snowman fantasy with your child in the recommendations that follow.

READINGS

The Snowman by Raymond Briggs (Random)

This wordless picture book depicts one little boy's fantasy come true, when his snowman comes to life at the stroke of midnight. Raymond Briggs needs no words to tell a story. His illustrations masterfully tell it all.

(*The Snowman* is also available as a videotape and film. It is exceptionally well-made. If you are able to see it with your child, look for all the additions in the movie as compared to the book and discuss them with your child.)

Our Snowman by M.B. Goffstein (Harper & Row)

A girl and her little brother build a snowman after the first blizzard of the season, but are sad to see it so lonely once they go inside. Daddy comes up with a solution to please everyone.

Kate's Snowman by Kay Chorao (Dutton)

When Kate, the elephant, wakes up to see it has snowed, she readies herself to go out to make a snowman. She has a vision of exactly what it will look like, but the end result turns out slightly different from what she had planned.

RECITINGS

MARY HAD A BIG SNOWMAN
(Sung to "Mary Had a Little Lamb")

Mary had a big snowman,
Big snowman, big snowman,
Mary had a big snowman
That she built in her back yard.

And every time she played outside,
Played outside, played outside,
Every time she played outside,
Her snowman was cold and hard.

But then one day the sun did shine,
Sun did shine, sun did shine,
Then one day the sun did shine,
So warm and bright and strong.

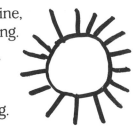

So Mary had to say goodbye,
Say goodbye, say goodbye,
Mary had to say goodbye,
Good-bye, friend, and so long.

WHERE, OH WHERE HAS MY GREAT SNOWMAN GONE?
(Sung to "Where, Oh Where Has My Little Dog Gone?")

Oh, where, oh where has my great snowman gone?
Oh where, oh where can he be?
With his big black eyes and his carrot nose,
Oh where, oh where can he be?

I made him after a big snowstorm.
We had two feet of fresh snow.
I rolled and rolled and made three round balls
And piled them up just so.

He looked so proud standing nice and tall.
He greeted all on our street.
My friends and neighbors, cats, dogs, and birds—
They all thought he was so neat.

I should have known that the day would come
When we'd have to say our goodbyes;
The sun was shining so brilliantly,
I should have realized.

Now all that's left is a big wet spot.
Did he soak down into the ground?
I like to think of him under there,
Romping happily all around.

RECIPES

SNOWMAN CAKE
Almost too good-looking to eat.

Grease and flour 2 round cake pans, one 8-inch pan and one 9-inch pan. Prepare any cake recipe you wish, whether it is a family favorite or a box cake. Divide the batter evenly between the two pans. Bake as your recipe directs.
Frost with the frosting below.

CREAMY FROSTING
1. Beat until light and fluffy 1/4 cup margarine and 2 egg yolks.
2. Add 1 teaspoon vanilla, 1/4 cup evaporated milk, and a dash of salt.
3. Beat well. Then gradually add 3 1/2 cups sifted powdered sugar, mixing until desired consistency is reached.

And now for the fun part: On whatever dish you have that is large enough (or on foil-covered cardboard), place the 8-inch layer for the head of the snowman and the 9-inch layer for the body. Frost the layers and join them together. Sprinkle them with flaked coconut. Adorn the snowman with assorted nuts, raisins, and dried fruit for eyes, mouth, buttons, and the like.

SNOWBALL COOKIES
1. Combine 1 1/2 cups finely chopped dried apricots and 2 cups shredded coconut. You can substitute 1/2 cup raisins for 1/2 cup apricots, for a different blend.
2. Add 2/3 cup sweetened condensed milk and blend well.
3. Shape into balls and roll in more coconut or powdered sugar.
4. Refrigerate until firm.

ACTIVITIES

BUILD YOUR OWN SNOWMEN
Snowman Tips
Go outside and build a snowman. Work on it together with your child. When the time comes for adorning the snowman with facial features and clothing, let your child's imagination take over. Take a photograph of the final product with your child standing proudly next to him, for a keepsake that will be loved long after the snowman melts away.

A Snowman for the Birds
After you have made your wonderful snowman, dress him in an old scarf and hat. Use sturdy twigs

to make arms and stick them on either side of the middle snowball. Now add the following things to turn this snowman into a special treat for the birds: For eyes, use prunes, peanuts, grapes, crackers, or banana slices. For a nose, use a carrot. To make buttons, fill small, empty bottle caps with peanut butter mixed with birdseed. Place the buttons on the snowman's body, with the peanut butter facing out.

As an extra treat for the birds, make snowman feeders. Take two empty grapefruit halves. Thread a 12-inch piece of string through the bottom of each half and tie a knot on the outside of the grapefruit half. Then fill each grapefruit half with cereal, bread crumbs, and/or raisins and tie the top of the string to the snowman's twig arms.

FELT SNOWMAN PUPPET

Take two pieces of white felt and cut out a snow-man shape large enough for your child's hand to fit inside (remember to add an inch or so to allow for sewing around the edges).

From scraps of materials, buttons, lace, or felt have your child pick out choices for the snowman's eyes, nose, mouth, scarf, and buttons. Cut the scraps, if necessary, to the desired shapes and sizes. Allow your child to glue on these pieces to one of the snowman-shaped pieces.

Sew the two pieces together, leaving an opening for the hand at the bottom edge. Let your child help with the sewing if he is able.

When the puppet is all sewn, create a skit with your child. For extra fun, make yourself a snow-man puppet, too, and double your child's fun act-ing out snowman fantasies.

SNOWSTORM IN A JAR

Your child can do this one all on her own.

Give her a paper punch, white paper, and a small jar full of water. Have her punch as many holes as she wants, put them in the jar, fasten the lid on tightly, and shake: snowstorm in a jar!

A "SHARECROW" FOR SNOW-LESS CLIMATES

If snows are few and far between where you live, you can still have fun with out-door wintertime creations.

Begin by constructing a simple frame for the Sharecrow's body. This is most simply done by tying or taping together a cross of two sticks. If you're not intimi-dated by more complicated handiwork, use a 6-foot piece of wood for the length; nail a 3-foot piece of wood 1½ feet down from the top for the shoulders; and nail a 2-foot piece of wood 3 feet down from the top for the hips.

Once you've built the frame, let your child's imagination take over as she dresses the Sharecrow. An old hat, shirt, gloves, tie, pants, and belt are fun to work with.

Put your Sharecrow in the yard where it can be viewed clearly from inside your house. Hang Snowman Feeders (see the activity above) and other birdseed treats from its arms and enjoy watching birds come to eat—as you share treats with them instead of scaring them away!

CHAPTER TWO

FEBRUARY

A Month Short on Days— Not on Fun

February may be the shortest month of the year, but that doesn't mean there is less time for fun. A great deal of fun can be squeezed into twenty-eight or twenty-nine days!
Your child will like exploring the unique qualities that make him who he is. You will both enjoy the playful suggestions for celebrating Valentine's Day. Both of you can relax on an imaginary getaway, and then make his bathtime something out of the ordinary.
Just as much energy and playfulness can be packed into this month as into the rest of the year!

FIRST WEEK

Feeling Good About "Me"

If you were to ask your child whom he loved, perhaps his reply would sound something like this: "I love Mommy, Daddy, Michael, Matthew, Kyle . . ." and he'd continue to list every aunt, uncle, cousin, neighbor, friend, and animal he'd ever met. This is wonderful. We want our children to be full of love for others. But whom did he neglect to mention? The most important person in his entire life—himself. A child needs to feel good about himself. He needs to be his own best buddy. Having a strong self-image doesn't just happen, it needs to be nurtured. With encouragement and praise a child's feeling of self-worth develops and grows.

As parents we have a responsibility to provide certain things for our children—food, clothing, and shelter, as well as an atmosphere that allows our children to grow up feeling both loved and worthy of our love. And what better time to have them zero in on their uniqueness and encourage them to feel good about themselves than the week before Valentine's Day? This chapter's self-awareness activities will help you help your child see just how special he is.

READINGS

Quick as a Cricket by Audrey Wood (Playspaces)

This book, with its bold and splashy illustrations, takes a child into a world of feelings and self-awareness and helps identify all the opposing emotions she may experience.

The 329th Friend by Marjorie Weinman Sharmat (Macmillan)

In an attempt to find someone who will like him, Emery Raccoon invites 328 guests to lunch. But after all the preparations and work, he finds one more, very surprising friend, one that he's had all the time.

The Mixed-up Chameleon by Eric Carle (Crowell Junior Books)

A small green chameleon visits a zoo and wishes to be like all the other animals he sees there. With each wish he changes somewhat until he is terribly mixed up. When he sees a fly but finds that he is unable to eat it in his new mixed-up body, he realizes just how pleasing it is to be himself.

RECITINGS

WHEN I'M . . .
(Sung to "Yankee Doodle")

When I'm sad, I want to cry—
At times I don't know why,
But usually I'm happy
With a sparkle in my eye.

Chorus:
(Michael Brennan), that is me,
(Michael Brennan), yes indeed!
I've got feelings, so do you,
Happy and sad are just a few.

(Substitute your child's name where "Michael Brennan" appears.)

When I'm shy I want to hide
Away from everybody,
But when I'm proud I'm very loud
And tell everybody.

(Chorus)

When I'm mad I stomp and yell
I mope around and shrug,
But most times I am loving
And want to kiss and hug.

(Chorus)

PEOPLE SAY
(Sung to "See-Saw, Marjorie Daw")

People say when they look at me
I look just like my mother.
I've got her eyes,
I've got her smile,
And my nose is like my father's.

And people say when they listen to me
I sound just like my sister.
My laugh, my cry,
My hellos and goodbyes,
Even my shouts and whispers.

But I can say
That it's okay
To look and sound like others.
I'm me inside,
And full of pride,
And that's what really matters!

RECIPES

"ME" PRETZELS
Easy, delicious, and personally yours.
1. Preheat oven to 425 degrees.
2. Dissolve 1 tablespoon yeast in $\frac{1}{2}$ cup warm water. Let sit for 5 minutes.
3. Add 1 teaspoon honey and 1 teaspoon salt.
4. Add $1\frac{1}{3}$ cups flour and knead until well-blended.
5. Roll small pieces between your hands into $\frac{1}{2}$-inch ropes and form letters—perhaps initials, all the letters in your child's name, or even the word *ME.*
6. Brush with beaten egg.
7. Bake 10 minutes at 425 degrees. Depending on the size of the letters you make, this recipe will yield about one dozen letters.

EGG Mc"ME"
This sandwich (besides being tasty) is distinctive because it can be named after your child. Instead of the "ME" in the name, insert your child's name, so it can be called, for example, Egg McMary.

1. Toast an English muffin and lightly butter it.
2. Fry one egg according to your child's liking.
3. Place the egg on top of one half of the English muffin, top with one slice of American cheese followed by a thin slice of ham (optional), and then add the other half of the English muffin.

THIS IS KRISTIN   THIS IS MY CAT   MITCH

ACTIVITIES

"ME" BOOK

To celebrate your child's uniqueness make a book together all about her. It doesn't matter whether you use white paper and crayons, or colored construction paper and ink; whether you staple, glue, or paper-clip the pages—use whatever materials you are most comfortable with and have available to you. What does matter is the subject you are writing about. Here are some ideas to get you started. Use one sentence or thought on each page.

This is me.
This is my family.
This is my house.
This is my pet.
This is my teacher.
My favorite book is _____.
My favorite food is _____.
My favorite color is _____.
My favorite toy (or game) is _____.
I feel happy when _____.
I feel sad when _____.
I feel brave when _____.
I feel shy when _____.
I feel strong when _____.
I feel weak when _____.

For each page that you do, your child can draw her own illustration. She can add photographs and clippings from magazines, too.

If you choose to do all of these suggested pages, or add more of your own, you may wish to do this project in several sessions.

"ME" OUTLINE

Take a piece of heavy paper large enough to trace your child's entire body. (Three to four grocery bags cut open and taped flat work well.) Lay it on the floor; have your child lie on her back on top of it and trace around her body. Let her color it however she wishes to show "what she is made up of." If she needs some ideas, try colors that represent the way she feels; colors that represent an animal she feels like; favorite colors; true colors of her hair, eyes, and favorite clothing.

"ME" PUPPET

Using an old sock, a paper bag, a paper plate, felt, or other material that you cut out, make a puppet with your child that will be representative of him. Have him plan the puppet's features to resemble himself. The eyes should be his eye color; the hair should be the color, length, and texture of his own hair; have him make a mouth in a big wide smile if he is happy (or however he is feeling). Continue in this fashion, making the puppet uniquely like your child. If you have more than one child, this is a good project for all your children to do. When each child has a "ME" puppet, each will gain self-confidence, and the play opportunities are numerous.

SECOND WEEK

Valentine's Day—a Well-Loved Holiday

What makes Valentine's Day such a well-loved holiday? Love. Everyone, no matter how young or old, gregarious or shy, wants to love and be loved. And on Valentine's Day everyone has a fair shot at it. Valentine love can come secretly, in the form of an unknown secret admirer, or openly, in the form of your close relatives or dearest friends. Valentine love can come modestly, in the form of a simple handmade paper heart, or love elaborately, in the form of a fancy, triple-layer, double-fudge, heart-shaped cake. Whatever form your valentine love comes in, make sure it comes to your loved ones. In this chapter you'll find suggestions for many different things to make and do for a Valentine's Day party.

READINGS

It's Valentine's Day by Jack Prelutsky (Greenwillow; pb Scholastic)

This comical collection of valentine poems will delight anyone and everyone who reads it. From "My Special Cake," where a little boy decides to create a cake to celebrate the holiday, to "I Made a Giant Valentine," where a little girl ends up giving her giant valentine to someone unexpected, to "My Father's Valentine," where a little boy attempts to cut out the "perfect" valentine heart for his daddy, you'll be entertained and find yourself laughing out loud.

One Zillion Valentines by Frank Model (Greenwillow)

Marvin and Milton learn a lot about valentines and making people happy during their inventive holiday preparations.

The Best Valentine in the World by Marjorie Weinman Sharmat (Holiday House)

On November 5 Ferdinand the Fox begins his Valentine's Day preparations. He wants to make Florette a very special valentine. But when Valentine's Day comes, a slight misunderstanding *almost* ruins the true love of the holiday.

RECITINGS

JACK LOVES JILL
(Sung to "Jack and Jill")
Jack loves Jill,
But Jill loves Bill,
And Bill says he loves Kara.
Kara's shy,
Says she loves Guy,
And Guy says he loves Sara.
Sara says
That Kyle's the best—
"I want him to be mine."
But Kyle loves me,
And I'm happy
To be his valentine!

DO YOU KNOW MY VALENTINE?
(Sung to "The Muffin Man")

Do you know my valentine,
The one that I choose to be mine?
She (he) is the best friend of mine,
If you know, put her (his) name on this line!

_____.

RECIPES

FANCY HEART SANDWICHES

Make your child's favorite sandwich, such as egg salad, peanut butter, cheese, or tuna fish.

Using a heart-shaped cookie cutter, cut the sandwich out.

Serve with slices of cucumber, celery, or carrot arranged decoratively around the outside of the sandwich.

SWEETHEART VALENTINE CAKE

1. Make a batter for your favorite cake, homemade or from a mix.
2. Pour the batter into one 9-inch round pan and one 9-inch square pan.
3. Bake according to the directions you have.
4. When the cakes are cooled, assemble them as follows: Cut the round cake in half. Take the square cake and place it on a large tray or serving dish. Angle it so that it is like a diamond. Put the two half-circles on either side of the top point of the square cake to make a heart shape.
5. Frost the cake using your favorite frosting.
6. Decorate as you wish.

VALENTINE PARTY

Invite some of your child's friends over for a Valentine's Day party. Your child and you can decorate the kitchen with Heart Streamers and make a Valentine Tree (directions below) to put in the center of the kitchen table for a festive look.

Serve the Fancy Heart Sandwiches with cut-up vegetables, a red punch such as cranberry-apple juice, and the Sweetheart Cake for dessert.

After lunch your child and her friends can play Hearty Actions and the Lub Dub Game, both described in the activities below.

Of course, let the children exchange valentines with each other and have a loving-good time!

ACTIVITIES

PARTY DECORATIONS
Heart Streamers

Use red construction paper. Cut into 3-by-12-inch strips. This should give you three strips from one piece of standard construction paper.

Direct your child to fold the strip in half once lengthwise, then in half again. Have her cut the top and bottom to form a heart, leaving about an inch of each folded side intact.

When she unfolds the strip she'll have four hearts all joined together.

Make more, if she wishes, to decorate walls, doors, and the like.

Valentine Tree

Find a full limb of a tree that has many small branches on it and bring it inside. Set it in a container that will hold it erect. (One possibility is an empty coffee can that you fill with pebbles or marbles. Put the lid on tightly and cut a hole in the lid just the right size to fit the limb inside.) Stick the branch into the container. Have your child cut out valentines from red, pink, and/or white construction paper. Tape a piece of string to each valentine. Tie the valentines to the tree branch. This makes a great centerpiece for your party table.

PARTY GAMES
Hearty Actions

Cut out a heart for each player. Think of various actions, such as jumping, galloping, crawling, hopping, and skipping. Write one action on each heart.

When you are ready to play, have everyone get in a circle.

Put the pile of hearts in the middle of the circle.

Select an order. Have the first player run up to the pile and take a heart. Without telling what the action is, he begins doing it. The others join in as soon as they can identify what they are to do. When all have returned to their original spots, they all sit down.

Then the next player runs up, chooses a heart, and leads everyone with her action. The game continues until everyone has had a turn to lead.

The Lub Dub Game

1. Seat all players on the floor in a circle.
2. While everyone chants "Lub Dub," have a leader make various hand signals for everyone to copy. For example, the leader may demonstrate the following sequence: touch your heart twice, clap your hands twice, touch your knees twice, rub your head twice, hit the floor twice, touch your shoulders twice.
3. Have the leader start off slowly, giving everyone time to catch on and follow. Then gradually increase the speed until one player remains, or until all are in a heap, giggling.

THIRD WEEK

An Island Getaway

"A few morning flurries will give way to partial clearing with temperatures rising into the fifties. Tonight rain is expected, heavy at times, with winds blowing from the northwest up to fifty miles per hour. Tomorrow there is a seventy-five percent chance of a major snowstorm dumping eight to ten inches of fresh snow on us. But by evening, all will have cleared up and temperatures will dip into the single digits."

Sound familiar? Even though this fabricated weather report is slightly exaggerated, sometimes winter weather can be crazy. The only certain thing about the weather is that it will change.

Have you had enough of it? Would you like to get away from it all? Escape to an imaginary island and bask in the warm climate you and your child create. Below are plans to get you started.

READINGS

The Island of the Skog by Steven Kellogg (Dial Books for Young Readers)

When Jenny and her fellow mice friends realize that they've had one narrow escape from the butcher's cat too many, they make plans to sail away to a peaceful island where mice can be free. Their trip, although a success, is not without problems. Steven Kellogg's humorous illustrations and clever story line make this adventure a treasure to be read over and over again.

Time of Wonder by Robert McCloskey (Viking)

If you've ever wondered what it would be like to spend an entire summer on an island, this book will tell you. From the early morning fog lifting to the preparations for and arrival of a fierce hurricane, Robert McCloskey describes everything so you feel as if you are there.

Island Winter by Charles Martin (Greenwillow)

As all of Heather's summer friends leave at the end of the season, she wonders how she'll spend the whole winter on the island. But she is amazed to see how much fun she can have and how quickly the winter months pass.

RECITINGS

ROW TO THAT ISLAND
(Sung to "Row, Row, Row Your Boat")

Row, row, row your boat,
Let's get away from here—
Escape from weather cold and bleak—
There's nothing we should fear.

Row, row, row your boat
To that island over there.
Once we reach it you will see
We haven't any cares.

Row, row, row your boat—
Soft breezes I can feel,
Warm sunshine beats on my face—
These feelings seem so real.

Row, row, row your boat—
Step out onto the sand.
Seashells blanket all around—
Hurrah! We've reached our land.

GO 'ROUND AND 'ROUND THE ISLAND
(Sung to "Go 'Round and 'Round the Village")

Go 'round and 'round the island,
Go 'round and 'round the island,
Go 'round and 'round the island
To see what I can see.

I see some shells and starfish,
I see some shells and starfish,
I see some shells and starfish
And more treasures for me.

I feel the sunshine warm me,
I feel the sunshine warm me,
I feel the sunshine warm me
And love the way it feels.

I love our pretend island,
I love our pretend island,
I love our pretend island
And wish that it was real!

RECIPES

ROLLED SANDWICHES

Use a rolling pin to flatten out a piece of whole wheat bread. Spread peanut butter, egg salad, or whatever you'd like on the bread. Roll the bread up and then roll it in waxed paper to save for your island getaway picnic, below. Remember this is equivalent to only half a sandwich, so make sure you pack enough to satisfy all the hungry travelers.

BITES OF SUNSHINE

Soften 4 envelopes of unflavored gelatin in ³/₄ cup pineapple juice. Add to this 1 cup boiling water. Add ¹/₄ cup sugar and 1 cup orange juice. Chill in a 9-by-9-inch pan, then cut into bite-sized pieces. Refrigerate in a covered container until you're ready to go.

ISLAND GETAWAY

Planning and packing for a pretend getaway with your child can sometimes be as much fun as the actual trip.

Make the above-mentioned recipes and pack them in a cooler, along with fruit juice, fresh fruit (strawberries or other summer fruit would be fun if affordable and available), napkins and paper plates, and a tablecloth or blanket for your picnic spread.

Pull out of the closets summer toys, balls, sunglasses, swimming suits, and other such items that will help give the feeling of a warm summer day at the beach.

Once you've made the sunshine, sailboat, and seashell activities mentioned below, you'll be ready to set sail for your island getaway!

Climb aboard your homemade sailboat (directions below) with your sunshine, toys, and lunch in hand. Take turns being navigator and captain; then decide when the time is right to exclaim, "Land ho!" Wade ashore however you and your crew see fit and begin your fun day in the sun. Hang up your sun, play with the sand toys you've brought, spread out your blanket, and have lunch. After lunch you may all want to have some seashell fun, as described in the activities below.

ISLAND GETAWAY PREPARATIONS

Sunshine: As this is one of the key ingredients, make sure you bring a lot. Get a large piece of poster board or other cardboard. Cut out as big a sun as you can. Have your child color it yellow and draw on a smiling face. Bring along masking tape to hang your sun when you get to your destination.

Sailboat: Use your creativity and imagination here. You'll need to make a boat large enough to seat yourself, your crew, and your supplies. Some suggestions: an arrangement of couch cushions and pillows; a large sheet spread out on the floor in the shape of a boat; masking tape placed on the floor to mark off a boat shape (remember, masking tape might leave a residue if left for too long a time).

Seashells: Cut various shapes and sizes of shells out of poster board or other firm cardboard. Clam and scallop shells would be good for this project. Make at least one for each person.

SEASHELL FUN

To make decorated seashells you'll need

■ 1 poster-board "shell" for each person
■ crayons or felt-tipped markers
■ assorted tiny shells, stones, starfish
■ small ornaments such as pearls, colored plastic pieces, sequins
■ glue

Let your child decorate the poster board "shells" by coloring them; then glue on the other items.

Many of these materials are available in craft shops or department stores if you don't have any saved from past beach trips.

Have a seashell hunt: Everyone loves treasure hunts, and this one will be a great way to end a wonderful getaway. Take turns hiding the "shells" around your "island." See if you can find them all every time; perhaps you can time each other to see how long it takes you to find the shells, too.

FOURTH WEEK

Bathtime—A Fun-filled Adventure

Water is a versatile substance. For starters it can be poured, frozen, or evaporated; some things will float on top of it, some will sink under it, and others will dissolve into it. We can cook, clean, and play with it and in it. And to children, that is the most exciting quality of water—for it is a limitless play medium.

The first and most obvious place for a child to enjoy water play is in the bathtub. With a myriad of toys or tools a child can become so involved in her water world that she may emerge hours later all "drimpled" up like a prune. So spread out the activities among several bathtimes. Baths aren't just for getting clean. A bath is a built-in science lab right in your own house. Allow plenty of time for your child to experiment with the amazing qualities of water. In this section you'll find some simple water play toys as well as some different things to augment your child's bathtime fun.

Bear in mind that "lifeguarding" whenever a child is in water is essential. Don't take her water skills for granted!

READINGS

King Bidgood's in the Bathtub by Audrey Wood (Harcourt Brace Jovanovich)

When King Bidgood refuses to get out of the bathtub his entire court tries to coerce him out. The king cannot be tricked by his knight, queen, duke, or court, but his clever page knows just what to do! This elaborately illustrated bathtime story was a 1986 Caldecott Honor Book.

No Bath Tonight by Jane Yolen (Harper Junior Books)

A little boy avoids taking a bath for an entire week because of the great "excuses" he has. It isn't until his grandmother tells him about reading "kid tea leaves" that he willingly jumps into the tub.

Harry, the Dirty Dog by Gene Zion (Harper Junior Books; pb Harper Trophy Books)

Harry absolutely hates taking baths. One day in an attempt to escape any more baths he decides to run away. As the day goes on he gets dirtier and dirtier until no one can even recognize him (including his own family when he decides to return home).

RECITINGS

RING AROUND THE BATHTUB
(Sung to "Ring around a Rosy")
Ring around the bathtub,
My mommy says I must scrub,
Three months have lapsed
Without a bath,
So now I really have to scrub.
One hour in the bathtub,

I soak and try to scrub,
The water's brown,
My skin, I've found,
Gets lighter every time I rub.

Two hours in the water.
Try soap? I think I ought'er,
The soap will get
Some dirt, I bet,
Hidden way down under.

I've been in here three hours,
I'm starting to smell like flowers,
I look so good,
I think I should
Plan a monthly shower!

SPLASH, SPLASH, SPLASH
(Sung to "Row, Row, Row Your Boat")

Splash, splash, splash around,
A bath is so much fun.
Bubbles, boats, soap, and floats—
Rinse and then I'm done.

RECIPES

Although these boats are not really "sailable," what an appropriate snack for before or after a playful bath.

EGG-BOATS

Peel a hard-boiled egg; cut it in half. Remove yolk and mix with 1 tablespoon plain yogurt and celery seed, dill, or other herbs to taste. Cut 2 small triangular pieces out of a pepper for sails; stick a toothpick into each one. Mound the yolk mixture into the egg halves, then stick in the pepper-on-a-stick sails.

MELON-BOATS

Cut one wedge out of a cantaloupe or other melon and discard the seeds. Stick a long thin pretzel into the center of the wedge as a mast. Add two triangular pieces of apple or pear on each side of the pretzel mast, securing them with toothpicks. Take three blueberries or grapes and stick them on a toothpick to be the "sailors." Stand them up wherever there is room on the melon wedge.

ORANGE-BOATS

Cut an orange in half, scoop out the pulp carefully without damaging the skin shell, and mix the orange pulp with pineapple tidbits, mandarin oranges, peaches, or other fruit. Spoon mixture back into the orange halves. Cut triangular pieces of banana, apple, pear, or other firm fruit, attach to a toothpick and insert one or two in the center of the orange as masts. Serve at once.

PEACH-BOATS

Sprinkle 1 envelope of Knox gelatin over 1/4 cup cold cranberry juice; let stand for 3 to 4 minutes. Add 3/4 cup cranberry juice, heated to boiling, and stir until gelatin is completely dissolved. Add 1 cup of any cut-up fruit except fresh pineapple. Chill until thickened slightly. Fill canned peach halves with the mixture. Use a carrot shaving on a toothpick as a sail and stick it into the boat shell. Chill in the refrigerator until gelatin mixture is firm.

ACTIVITIES

BATHTIME PLAY IDEAS

Chances are your child doesn't need to have anything with her when she takes a bath other than her imagination. But the following list of everyday items can add to her fun and help her create even more imaginative situations.

Various sized measuring cups and spoons, sponges, corks, straws, washcloths, egg beater, eye dropper, ping-pong balls, funnels, meat baster, ladle, watering can, strainer, plastic squeeze bottles, bowls, spray pump bottles, boats, soap, a Waterlens, and a Waterscope (see "Fireflies" in Chapter Seven). Some of these may lead to watery splashes in all directions, so be prepared or be selective. If you keep the water level low in the tub, you'll minimize any messiness.

SOAPFLOATS

Give your child a bar of Ivory soap (Ivory works well because it floats and is soft enough to stick other things into it). Discuss what he wants to make. Remember that the bar of soap is the center of the float. Provide some kind of soft plastic (like coffee can lids), aluminum foil, or other waterproof material. From these your child can cut out pieces and shapes that will add to his float, stick the pieces into the soap, and when it is all arranged, float his creation in the water. For example, to make a turtle, he can cut a head, four little legs, and a tail out of plastic, stick them into the soap in the appropriate places, and let the soapy turtle float with him in the bathtub.

BUBBLE BATH BLOWER

Since bubbles are a big part of bathtime fun, try making this homemade blower to add even more bubbles. First, have your child cut a small square out of an old washcloth or other terry cloth material large enough to cover the top of a small paper cup. (You may need to help with the cutting.) Secure the cloth over the top of the cup with a rubber band. Make a little hole in the side of the cup and insert a straw into the hole. Make a small mixture of water and bubble bath. Dip the cloth part of the blower into the mixture. When he blows through the straw he should get lots of bubbles!

CHAPTER THREE

MARCH
A Month of Magic

Parades, music, kites, and dinosaurs can captivate people time after time. I have attended dozens of parades and have yet to tire of the sight of marching bands and fancy floats. I have listened to thousands of songs and am still moved when listening to any quality musical performance. I have flown many kites and continue to feel uplifted each time I set one aloft. And I have studied dinosaurs for several years with my children but find that I am still thirsting to learn even more about them.

All these subjects have some allure that keeps people's interest steady. During this month when the weather is everything but magical, enjoy some of the magic offered in this chapter.

FIRST WEEK

When Irish Eyes Are Smiling

One day in March you may feel that you are looking at the world through green-tinted glasses. Don't panic—check your calendar—it's St. Patrick's Day! This is a day when everyone, no matter what nationality, is a little Irish . . . a day when everything from bagels to fresh carnations is green . . . a day when Irish-Americans celebrate their heritage with Irish symbols like shamrocks, harps, and shillelaghs. This is a day for big festive parades with hundreds of marchers playing bagpipes, wearing kilts, and honoring the Emerald Isle for its rich traditions. Broaden your child's horizons and help make this St. Patrick's Day more meaningful as you plan your own St. Patrick's Day parade, complete with flags, decorations, and Irish food.

READINGS

St. Patrick's Day in the Morning by Eve Bunting (Clarion Books)

Jamie Donovan is considered too young to march in the St. Patrick's Day parade. To prove that he is big enough to complete the entire parade route, Jamie sets out in the early morning hours to march the route himself. As he does, readers are treated to picturesque descriptions and drawings of the Irish countryside. This book is not only a story of one little lad's determination, but it's also a beautiful Irish travelogue from our personal tour-guide, Jamie.

Jeremy Bean's St. Patrick's Day by Alice Schertle (Lothrop, Lee & Shepard Books)

Jeremy is excited about St. Patrick's Day. His class is planning a party complete with green pickles, cupcakes, and apples to celebrate the approaching holiday. But on the actual day Jeremy's happiness is almost ruined until a new unexpected friend saves the day.

Little Bear Marches in the St. Patrick's Day Parade by Janice Brustlein (Lothrop, Lee & Shepard Books)

It is St. Patrick's Day and the annual parade will have to be canceled because of the terrible rainy weather. Everyone is sad until Little Bear shows up and causes the show to go on.

RECITINGS

CLAIRE IS WEARING GREEN TODAY
(Sung to "Mary Had a Little Lamb")

Claire is wearing green today,
Green today, green today.
Claire is wearing green today
For it's St. Patrick's Day.

And Kyle is wearing green today,
Green today, green today.
Kyle is wearing green today
For it's St. Patrick's Day.

Add other names of family and friends and continue in the same fashion.

HAVE YOU SEEN A LEPRECHAUN?
(Sung to "Do You Know the Muffin Man?")

Have you seen a leprechaun,
A leprechaun, a leprechaun—
Have you seen a leprechaun,
So magical and green?

I've heard he has a pot of gold,
A pot of gold, a pot of gold.
I've heard he has a pot of gold
But this I've never seen.

So if you find a leprechaun,
A leprechaun, a leprechaun—
If you find a leprechaun
Catch him and bring him to me.

RECIPES

Corned beef, cabbage, and boiled potatoes make a traditional Irish meal. Below is a less familiar but tasty Irish menu you may serve for St. Patrick's Day dinner.

IRISH LAMB STEW
1. Roll 2 pounds of cubed lamb pieces in 3 tablespoons flour seasoned with 1/2 teaspoon salt and 1/4 teaspoon pepper.
2. Brown the lamb pieces in 2 tablespoons margarine.
3. Put 1 1/2 cups hot water; 4 carrots, cut in 2-inch

pieces; 3 large potatoes, cubed; 3 stalks of celery, cut in 2-inch pieces; 1 bay leaf; 1/2 teaspoon dill seed; and 12 small white onions in a saucepan. Bring to a boil, then cover and simmer for 1 1/2 hours.
4. Add 1 10-ounce package of frozen peas and simmer for another 10 minutes.

Complete the meal with a green salad brimming with lettuce, green peppers, green olives, avocados, sprouts, broccoli, string beans, and anything else you can think of that is appropriately green!

You may also wish to make some Irish Soda Bread—a traditional, delicious bread that can be served with the meal, or even for breakfast the next morning lightly toasted with a little butter.

IRISH SODA BREAD
1. Preheat oven to 350 degrees.
2. Sift together 4 cups flour, 3 teaspoons baking powder, 1 teaspoon baking soda, 1/2 cup sugar, and 1/2 teaspoon salt in a large bowl.
3. Add 1 cup raisins and 3 tablespoons caraway seeds. (If you like, use 1/2 cup regular and 1/2 cup golden raisins.)
4. Blend in another bowl 3 well-beaten eggs, 1 1/2 cups milk, and 3 tablespoons oil.
5. Make a hole in the flour mixture and pour in the liquid mixture, stirring until smooth.
6. Bake for 1 hour in a large, round, greased pan. (A 9-inch cake pan will work fine.) Brush with egg yolk over the top for shine and crust.

For dessert, try green sherbet, pistachio ice cream, or sugar cookies cut out in the shape of shamrocks.

YOUR OWN
ST. PATRICK'S DAY PARADE

Many towns have a St. Patrick's Day Parade. You may wish to check local newspapers and television programming to see if there are going to be any parades. Whether there is one for you to attend or one for you to view on television, you can plan one of your own.

Rummage through closets and drawers and pull out as many green items as you can find to outfit your little Irish marcher.

Either find, borrow, or improvise some type of musical instruments to play while marching. (Harmonicas, makeshift drums/cymbals, wax-paper covered combs— anything will suffice as long as it makes "music.")

Make Irish Flags to carry (directions below).

Make Decorative Shamrocks to wear (directions below).

Make Irish-Green Corsages to wear (directions below).

When you have everything ready, let your parade begin. Carry this out to your own personal limit. March only from one room to the next, or don coats and hats (green, of course) and parade up and down your street.

IRISH FLAGS

Give your child a rectangular piece of white paper, whatever size you choose.

Hold it lengthwise and divide it into 3 equal sections.

Have your child color the left side section green, leave the middle section white, and color the right section orange.

Tape or staple a ruler, stick, or toothpick (depending on the size of your flag) to hold your flag.

DECORATIVE SHAMROCKS

Cut large shamrock shapes out of poster board or heavy white paper.

Let your child brush on diluted glue and then sprinkle one of the following over the glue: green glitter, green decorator sugars, or green rice (rice dyed with green food coloring).

Allow drying time, then shake off excess glitter, sugars, or rice.

IRISH-GREEN CORSAGES

Give your child white pompoms or white carnations to put in water with some green food coloring or green ink. As the water rises through the stems and petals, the flowers will turn green. (It may take up to 48 hours for this to happen.)

Tie pretty green ribbons around each flower's stem.

Use pins to fasten the corsages to coats, shirts, or sweaters.

SECOND WEEK

Music Magic

Music is so magical it can touch you no matter what your mood; so diverse it can please you no matter what your musical taste; and so universal it can communicate with you no matter what your native tongue.

Music is a wonderful medium to use with children. Whether your child will grow up to be an active performer or a passive listener, encourage him to develop a love for music. With the professional quality of children's performers on the rise (see Recordings below) and the interest in music education reaching all ages, there is no limit to the exciting activities and musical opportunities to which you can expose your child. Explore the magic of music together as you enjoy the following activities.

READINGS

Geraldine, the Music Mouse by Leo Lionni (Pantheon)

When Geraldine experiences music for the very first time, she is thrilled beyond words and knows that her life will never be the same.

Lentil by Robert McCloskey (The Viking Press)

Lentil is a young boy who loves music but can't sing or whistle a note. He buys a harmonica, learns to play it exceedingly well, and eventually becomes a hero playing it when every other musician is silenced.

The Banza by Diane Wolkstein (Dial)

On the island of Haiti, a little tiger named Teegra and a little goat named Cabree become best friends as a result of getting separated from their families during a thunderstorm. When Teegra is reunited with her family she gives Cabree a ***banza***—a little banjo that will protect Cabree forever.

RECITINGS

Help your child make up a song of his own. Use a familiar tune and then adapt new words to the tune. Here are two examples.

I LOVE MUSIC
(Sung to "Frère Jacques")

I love music, I love music.
Do you, too? Do you, too?
Drums, pianos, violins, horns, guitars, and mandolins
Are just a few. Just a few!

MATTHEW BRENNAN HAD A BAND
(Sung to "Old MacDonald Had a Farm")

Matthew Brennan had a band,
Ee-i, ee-i, oh.
And in his band he had some drums,
Ee-i, ee-i, oh.
With a tap, tap here
And a tap, tap there.
Here a tap, there a tap,
Everywhere a tap, tap.
Matthew Brennan had a band,
Ee-i, ee-i, oh.

Substitute your child's name in the song.
Continue with the following suggested verses:

- *Cymbals*—crash, crash
- *Trombone*—wah, wah
- *Flute*—tweet, tweet
- *Trumpet*—toot, toot

Add any other instruments you would like.

RECORDINGS

Recordings for children are definitely on the rise. Several really talented and wonderful musical groups are recording songs for children that are not only entertaining, but educational and thought-provoking as well. All recordings listed are available as long-playing albums as well as tape cassettes. At this writing, only a few are available as compact discs (including several of Raffi's), but expect more compact discs in the future. Keep your eyes (and ears) open for some of the following:

Dinosaurs, Dolphins and Dreams by Bank St.
Getting To Know Myself by Hap Palmer (or any other of his recordings)
One Light One Sun by Raffi (or any other of his recordings)
One, Two, Three, Four, Look Who's Coming Through the Door by Sharon, Lois & Bram (or any other of their recordings)
Reading Rainbow Songs by Steve Horelick
Really Rosie by Carole King
Share It by Rosenshontz (or any other of their recordings)
Space Songs by Tom Glazer (or any other of his recordings)
You'll Sing a Song and I'll Sing a Song by Ella Jenkins (or any other of her recordings)

RECIPES

CRUNCHY "DRUMSTICKS"

Although these drumsticks don't make good music, they surely do make for good eating.

1. Preheat oven to 375 degrees.
2. Place 2 beaten eggs in a bowl, and set aside. Put about 2 cups of flour in a plastic bag, and set aside. In another plastic bag, place 2 cups of corn flakes or potato chips. Close tightly. Use a rolling pin to crush them into small crumbs (especially fun for a child to do). Set this bag aside.
3. Pull the skin off 8 chicken drumsticks.
4. Coat each drumstick with flour by tossing it in the bag of flour.
5. Dip each floury drumstick into the bowl of beaten eggs.
6. Coat each drumstick with the crushed corn flakes or potato chips by tossing them in the plastic bag.
7. Put the drumsticks into a 13-by-9-by-2-inch baking pan and bake for about an hour, depending on the thickness of the drumsticks.

"FLUTE" COOKIES

These cookies may look like flutes, but when you bring them up to your lips I can guarantee they won't stop there!

1. In a large mixing bowl, beat ½ cup margarine till it is softened. Add ⅓ cup sugar, ¼ cup unsweetened cocoa powder, 1 egg, and 1 teaspoon vanilla. Beat until fluffy.
2. With mixer on slow speed, beat in ¼ cup water.
3. Gradually add 2 cups flour, beating till the mixture is well blended. Cover and chill dough until it is firm enough to handle, about 2 hours.
4. Preheat oven to 350 degrees. Divide dough into 12 equal pieces. On a lightly floured surface roll each part of the dough into a 12-inch rope. With a knife cut each rope into 3-inch sections.
5. Place short sections about 1 inch apart on un-greased cookie sheets. Lightly press 3 or 4 small candies, nuts, or pieces of dried fruit atop each cookie.
6. Bake for 12-15 minutes.
   Makes about 4 dozen "flutes."

ACTIVITIES

HOMEMADE TAMBOURINES

1. Give your child two paper plates to decorate as she wishes.
2. Place a few uncooked beans or macaroni inside one plate and cover it with the other plate turned upside down. Help to staple the plates securely together.
3. Encourage her to "play" the instrument tambourine-fashion to whatever music she chooses. If you want, suggest familiar tunes such as "Twinkle, Twinkle, Little Star" or "Baa Baa Black Sheep."

HOMEMADE GUITARS

1. Find a sturdy, low-sided box, such as a shoebox.
2. Have your child stretch rubber bands of varying lengths and widths over the box.
3. Let her strum and experiment with the different sounds she can make.

SOUND EXPERIMENTS

Once your child has made instruments, you can do the following activities:

1. Sit together. Try different ways to make loud sounds, then soft sounds. You can use the two instruments your child made, or anything else you wish to try. Some other possibilities are hand-clapping, feet-stomping, singing, talking, or using a recording, pans, or spoons.
2. If this is enjoyable, try to make sounds fast, and then slow; high and then low.

There are many musical experiments you can try, many musical games you can play. Let these be just a beginning.

THIRD WEEK

Kite Magic

Every child from age 1 to 100 thrills at the sight of a kite suspended against a glorious blue sky. What is it that makes kites so exciting? A kite is a signal of the arrival of warm spring days, a symbol of the free spirit in us all, and a challenge to conquer the power of gravity, all rolled into one. So on the next warm windy day take your home-made or store-bought kite, find a large enough clearing (where there are no kite-eating trees!), and experience the thrill of kite-flying together.

READINGS

Curious George Flies a Kite by H.A. Rey (Houghton Mifflin, Co.)

Curious George the monkey lives with the man with the yellow hat who is always telling George not to get into trouble. But George can't help it! In this adventure, among other escapades, George attempts to fly a kite that is twice his size. Luckily for him, the man with the yellow hat always arrives just in time to rescue poor George.

Merle the High-Flying Squirrel by Bill Peet (Houghton Mifflin, Co.)

Merle, a scrawny, timid squirrel, lives in the big city but dreams of living out west where the majestic redwoods grow. With the help of a high-flying kite Merle finds his redwoods and learns some valuable lessons in the process.

Fish in the Air by Kurt Wiese (The Viking Press)

A little Chinese boy named Fish asks his dad to buy him the biggest kite that looks like a fish. It is a very windy day when his dad buys it for him, and Fish gets a tremendous surprise from his new kite.

RECITINGS

MY BLUE-AND-PURPLE-STRIPED KITE
(Sung to "Incey Wincey Spider")

My blue-and-purple-striped kite climbed up into the sky.
Down came the rain, I felt like I would cry.
Out came the sun and dried up all the rain.
So my blue-and-purple-striped kite climbed into the sky again.

MY YELLOW KITE
(Sung to "London Bridge")

My yellow kite is great to fly,
Great to fly, great to fly.
My yellow kite is great to fly
And so much fun.

My yellow kite is sailing high,
Sailing high, sailing high.
My yellow kite is sailing high
As I jump and run.

My yellow kite's part of the sky,
Of the sky, of the sky.
My yellow kite's part of the sky,
Just like the sun.

My yellow kite is drifting down,
Drifting down, drifting down.
My yellow kite is drifting down—
Guess we're all done.

RECIPES

KITE BREAKFAST

Follow your favorite recipe for French toast. Once you've cooked it, cut it into a diamond shape and put it on a plate.

Next, cut a banana in half. Then slice it in fours the long way to get four thin strips. Put one strip at the bottom corner of the kite—this is the tail.

Use nuts or other fruit pieces, such as orange sections, halved grapes, or berries, to be the bows on the tail.

KITE LUNCH

You could do the same type of kite for a luncheon idea, by cutting a sandwich into a kite shape, then using spaghetti for the tail and cut-up fresh vegetables for the bows.

Add some kite snacks and desserts by cutting diamond-shaped pieces of cheese and fruit. Spear them with a straight pretzel.

Use your imagination and create more of your own kite foods.

ACTIVITIES

CRÊPE PAPER STREAMERS

This is the easiest kite to make. Simply give your child about a 4-foot strip of crêpe paper to do different things with. He may hold it in his hand and run with it to see the effects of the wind on it, throw it into the air and watch it fall, or tie it to various things outside and let it catch the breeze.

INDOOR KITE

This is a project to make but not to fly.

1. Take a piece of construction paper and cut a diamond shape out of it.

2. Have your child draw on it and glue small pieces of paper, foil, and other material to decorate it.
3. Help him punch a hole in one corner and attach a string to it for the tail.
4. Your child can add bows to the tail by adding small pieces of material. Again, encourage him to be creative, using a variety of materials and lots of splashy color.
5. Hang his kite from the ceiling, walls, or doors to bring the spring-like feeling indoors.

MAKE A REAL KITE

Kites are so inexpensive that making one really is not necessary. But if you should want to try to make one yourself, follow these nine steps and you'll have a kite ready to go. Decide which steps would be appropriate for your child to do and allow her participation whenever possible.

1. Lay a 28-inch stick across a 34-inch stick, 6 inches down from the top.
2. Glue and tie the sticks tightly together with twine.
3. Cut notches in the ends of the sticks.
4. Run string all the way around the outside edges of the kite through each notch. Wind it around each end a few times.
5. Lay the kite frame on wrapping paper. Cut the kite covering 2 inches bigger than the frame. Decorate the front of the kite however you'd like.
6. Fold the edges of the covering over the string and glue them down.
7. Make a bridle for your kite (on the front side). Tie a piece of string to both ends of each stick. Where they all meet, tie on a flying string.
8. Tie on a tail with some rags.
9. Wrap your flying string around a stick and go fly your kite.

FOURTH WEEK

Dinosaur Magic

There are varying degrees of dinosaur interest in children, ranging from mild curiosity to insatiable fascination. While one child's dinosaur knowledge might be limited to a general idea that dinosaurs were huge animals that lived a long time ago, another child might be able to rattle off the ten best-known dinosaurs, tell you whether they were carnivorous or herbivorous, state how many teeth they had, and expound even further about details few adults could recite.

Whether your child describes **Tyrannosaurus rex** as a "big animal" or as a "45 foot long, 20 foot tall, 8-ton king of all the dinosaurs," the subject of dinosaurs can not only be full of incredible information but a great deal of fun as well. The activities that follow can be adapted to suit your own child's level of interest.

READINGS

Dinosaurs—A Lost World by Keith Moseley (Putnam Publishing Group)

Dinosaurs almost come to life in this handsome pop-up book. Open one page and an **Allosaurus** skeleton unfolds before your eyes. Another page sends **Archaeopteryx** flying towards you. This book is full of information and excitement.

Patrick's Dinosaur by Carol Carrick (Clarion Books)

When Patrick and his older brother, Hank, go to the zoo, Hank starts comparing some of the animals to the true giants of the past—the dinosaurs. Patrick is afraid until he is convinced that all the dinosaurs died millions of years ago.

Also available by the same author on the subject of dinosaurs is **What Happened to Patrick's Dinosaurs?**

My Visit to the Dinosaurs by Aliki (Crowell Junior Books; pb Harper Junior Books)

This is a nice combination of an informational dinosaur book and a storybook. It weaves facts into a story about a little boy who visits a dinosaur museum with his family. Also available by the same author on the subject of dinosaurs are **Digging Up Dinosaurs** and **Dinosaurs Are Different.**

RECITINGS

WHERE HAVE THE DINOSAURS GONE?
(Sung to "Where, Oh Where Has My Little Dog Gone?")

Oh where, oh where have the dinosaurs gone?
Oh where, oh where can they be?
With their spikes and horns, and their fearful roars,
Oh where, oh where can they be?

Some people say that the earth got cold,
The dinosaurs moved so slow;
Whether cold, a comet, or something else,
We'll probably never know.

DID YOU EVER SEE A DINOSAUR?
(Sung to "Did You Ever See a Lassie?")

Did you ever see a dinosaur, a dinosaur, a dinosaur,
Did you ever see a dinosaur go this way and that?
They'd stomp and they'd chomp,
And they'd roar and much more—
Did you ever see a dinosaur go this way and that?

No, I never saw a dinosaur, a dinosaur, a dinosaur,
No, I never saw a dinosaur go this way and that.
I like to pretend, but I'm glad it's the end,
'Cause I'd never want to see one go this way or that!

RECIPES

STEGOSAURUS SALAD

Cut a pear in half from stem to bottom; scrape out the seeds and core.

Place one half, center down, on a plate. This is *Stegosaurus's* back.

Cut a line down the back; insert either almonds, banana chips, or pineapple pieces for *Stegosaurus's* bony plates.

Use a shelled peanut for the head.

Make a tail of raisins. At the end of the tail, pierce two raisins with four sunflower seeds to represent the four spikes in *Stegosaurus's* tail.

STUFFED BAKED POTATOSAUR

1. For each person you will be serving, bake one potato according to your usual method (two suggestions: prick the potatoes and bake for one hour at 400 degrees; or prick the potatoes, place them on a paper towel in a circle in a microwave oven, bake for eight minutes at high, then rotate the potatoes 180 degrees and continue baking for 8 more minutes.)
2. Let the potatoes cool enough for easier handling, and then cut open the top and scoop out the inside of the potato, leaving the bottom shell uncut.
3. For 6 potatoes: Mix the potato insides with 6 ounces of shredded cheese (choose one of your liking—cheddar, Swiss, and American are flavorful), 6 tablespoons of sour cream, 3 tablespoons melted margarine, and 1 bunch of steamed chopped broccoli (or other cooked vegetable). You may add seasonings (such as 1 teaspoon of dill or celery seed) and chopped meats (such as cubed ham, chicken, or turkey), if you'd like.
4. Stuff the potato shells with this mixture and mound the top to resemble *Stegosaurus, Dimetrodon,* or any other dinosaur you wish.
5. Bake the potatoes for another 10 minutes.

These recipes are offered to spark your own creative cooking minds! See what other dinosaur foods you can design.

ACTIVITIES

DINOSAUR SKELETONS

1. Draw a large dinosaur outline on 8½-by-11 inch paper by either tracing cookie cutters, tracing one from a picture, or drawing it freehand.
2. Give your child flat toothpicks. Have her dip them in glue and arrange them inside the dinosaur outline as the skeleton. Allow your child to do her own arrangement.
3. Let her add color with crayons if she wants.

DINOSAUR DIORAMAS

1. Give your child an empty shoebox, and have him stand it up on one of its long sides.
2. Help him draw, cut out, and decorate the background with trees, ferns, and volcanoes to make a suitable environment for his dinosaurs.
3. He can draw and cut out dinosaurs, or use any small dinosaur models you have on hand, to arrange in his diorama.

I'M THINKING OF . . .

Play the following game with your child after she has gotten to a point in her dinosaur "study" where she can successfully "show off" her knowledge.

Phrase your questions like riddles. For example—"I'm thinking of a dinosaur that was a plant eater and was the longest dinosaur of all" or "I'm thinking of a dinosaur that was a plant-eater that had three horns." *(Diplodocus* and *Triceratops)*

CHAPTER FOUR

APRIL
A Month Showering Delights

Certainly April showers bring May flowers, but there are other delights that the month of April rains upon us too. The Easter Bunny arrives with a basket filled with treats. National Library Week brings an opportunity to shower our children with glorious stories and books. These combine with the natural beauty blossoming outdoors to make April a delightful month to celebrate with your child.

FIRST WEEK

Easter Eggstravaganza

The season has arrived when people do such silly things with eggs. We color them, paint them, and dye them. We hide them and have treasure hunts with them. We cut out paper eggs, create papier-mâché eggs, and sculpt clay eggs. We buy egg-shaped chocolate, doughnuts, toys, and books. We hang plastic eggs from branches to make egg trees or fill them with miniature treasures of fruits, nuts, and candy.

The origins of all this "eggstravagance" date back to ancient times, when the decorated Easter egg was a symbol of renewed life—in a Christian sense, the resurrection of Jesus; in a natural or secular sense, the freshness of spring.

Whatever your reasons, be silly and have some foolish fun with eggs as you try the activities suggested below.

READINGS

The Country Bunny and the Little Gold Shoes by DuBose Heyward (Houghton Mifflin; pb Sandpiper)

Every bunny's lifelong dream is to be kind, swift, and wise enough to be someday chosen as an Easter bunny. This tender story, an Easter classic, tells of one country bunny's determination to achieve this goal. You might wish to read it in two sessions, as it has forty-eight pages and might be too lengthy for some children to finish in one sitting.

The Easter Egg Artists by Adrienne Adams (Charles Scribner's Sons; pb Atheneum)

The Abbots are Easter-egg-painting rabbits. Mr. and Mrs. Abbot are concerned about their son, Orson, and fear that he may not wish to join the family business. But once given time and space, Orson shows his creativity and talent.

The Great Big Especially Beautiful Easter Egg by James Stevenson (Greenwillow Books)

Here Grandpa, that inveterate hero of James Stevenson's creation, is at it again—weaving another fantastic tall tale about his childhood. This time he tells the adventure of trying to get the biggest, most beautiful Easter egg for his girlfriend, Charlotte.

RECITINGS

THE EASTER BUNNY'S COME
(Sung to "Frère Jacques")

Are you sleeping, are you sleeping,
Little one, little one?
The Easter Bunny's come,
It's time for hunting fun—
Wake up now, wake up now.

Are you sleeping, are you sleeping,

Little one, little one?
I see some chocolate eggs,
So jump up on your legs,
And let's have fun, let's have fun.

DROP GO THE EASTER EGGS
(Sung to "Pop Goes the Weasel")

All around the grassy lawn
The Easter Bunny hops along.
A pink egg here, a purple one there,
Drop! go the Easter eggs.

We're up and out at the break of dawn
To hunt for hidden treasures.
A pink egg here, a purple one there,
Yay! for the Easter eggs.

RECIPES

EASTER EGG COOKIES YOU CAN PAINT

1. Make a batch of your favorite sugar cookie dough or use this recipe:

   Mix $1/3$ cup margarine with $1/4$ cup sugar. Add 1 egg, $2/3$ cup honey, and $1/2$ teaspoon vanilla. Beat well. Combine $2^1/2$ cups flour, $1/4$ cup wheat germ, 1 teaspoon baking soda, and $1/4$ teaspoon salt. Gradually add to the butter mixture, beating well. Cover and chill at least 1 hour.
2. Preheat oven to 350 degrees. Grease cookie sheets. Roll dough out on a lightly floured surface to $1/4$-inch thickness. Cut the dough with an egg-shaped cookie cutter. (If you only have a round one, bend it slightly into an oval.)
3. Beat together 1 egg yolk, $1/4$ teaspoon water, and 2 or 3 drops of food coloring in a small bowl. Do this for each color you wish to use as paint. Using a clean paintbrush or Q-tip, paint designs onto your Easter egg cookies.

4. Bake for 6 to 8 minutes or until the cookies are golden.
   Makes 3 to 4 dozen cookies.

DEVILED EGGS

1. Hard-boil 4 eggs. Remove their shells, cut them in half lengthwise, and scoop out the yolks into a small bowl.
2. Mix the egg yolks with 1 tablespoon mayonnaise, $1/2$ teaspoon mustard, $1/2$ tablespoon pickle relish, $1/4$ teaspoon dill, and $1/4$ teaspoon celery seed.
3. Fill the egg halves with the yellow deviled egg mixture.
4. If you wish to change the color of the egg white for an even more festive look, first soak the egg whites in beet juice for 1 to 2 minutes before filling them with the deviled egg mixture. You will have pink deviled eggs!
   Makes 8 deviled eggs.

ACTIVITIES

EGG TREES
These trees can be beautiful indoor or outdoor decorations.

Indoor Tree
Choose a full limb of a tree that has many small branches on it and bring it inside. Set it in a container that will hold it erect. (For suggestions on

how to secure it, see the Valentine Tree in Chapter Two.)

Give your child plastic eggs and help him attach thread, string, or yarn to them. Do this by using tape or by opening the plastic eggs and stuffing part of the yarn inside before closing the egg up.

Let your child hang the eggs from the branches in decorative patterns, adding other festive decorations if he wishes.

Outdoor Tree

Prepare the eggs as suggested above and string them on your favorite tree outside.

WALKING EASTER EGG

1. Cut two large egg shapes out of butcher paper—large enough to sandwich your child.
2. Let your child decorate one side of each egg pattern.
3. Connect the front and back eggs by stapling, taping, and/or tying. Shoulder straps could be added, made out of string, cloth, paper, or tape. Cut the straps to size.

Use this costume when having an Easter Egg Hunt (see below) or at any other appropriate time.

EASTER EGG HUNT

This tradition is perhaps one of the most exciting of the holiday, and really can be done at any time of the year (and actually is—it's just known by another name: treasure hunt!).

1. Decide what kind of eggs you are going to hide and then prepare them. You can hard-boil and decorate your own, draw and cut some out of paper, buy plastic ones, or come up with any other egg ideas you can.
2. Take turns hiding and finding the eggs. Set up the boundaries and rules—for example, indoor hunts might be limited to certain rooms; outdoor hunts may be limited to certain areas.

EASTER EGG GAMES

Pass the Boiled Egg

This is similar to Musical Chairs. Have all the players sit in a circle. One egg is passed from player to player to the sound of music playing. When the music stops, whoever has the egg in his hand wins.

Egg Relay

Have two people race against each other. Each player must roll an egg across the floor from one designated spot to the other, using only his or her nose to roll it (or only blowing with a straw).

There are many more egg projects you can do. After all the hard-boiled eggs have served their decorative purposes, use the eggs in recipes and the crushed eggshells in art projects. (If you plan to eat the hard-boiled eggs, remember to refrigerate them, as they will spoil rather quickly.)

SECOND WEEK

Exploring a Local Gold Mine

There is a place in your community that offers a multitude of services, can accommodate infants through senior citizens, and has more treasures to offer than an untapped gold mine, all for free! Just prove that you are a resident in your town and you'll be issued a card that will make you a member of the richest gold mine of knowledge—your public library. Many of us take our libraries for granted; the countless books, toys, videotapes, games, records, programs and resources that are available to us are seldom even used.

The second week of April is National Library Week. Take time this week to appreciate this wonderful resource through the projects mentioned in this chapter.

READINGS

I Like the Library by Anne Rockwell (Dutton)
This book points out the many services a library offers, from books to records, story hours to puppet shows.

Petunia by Roger Duvoisin (Knopf)
Petunia, a silly goose, has heard that anyone who owns books and loves them is surely wise. So one day when she finds a book in the meadow, she decides to keep it and love it so that she can be truly wise. Unfortunately for Petunia and her friends, she learns the hard way that it takes more than merely holding a book under her wing to become wise.

Mike's House by Julia Lena Sauer (The Viking Press)
Robert loves going to Picture Book Hour at the library every week for many reasons, but especially because he gets to take a book home for the entire week. Robert always picks out *Mike Mulligan and His Steam Shovel* by Virginia Burton. He loves that book so much he calls the library "Mike's house." Robert never wants to miss going to Picture Book Hour, even when there is a blizzard, because he enjoys it so much. But one day he has quite a confusing adventure en route to the library that every reader will enjoy.

RECITINGS

WE'LL BE GOING TO THE LIBRARY, TODAY!
(Sung to "She'll Be Coming 'round the Mountain")

We'll be going to the library today, *(spoken)* Ya-hoo!

We'll be going to the library today, *(spoken)* Ya-hoo!

We'll be going to the library,
We'll be going to the library,
We'll be going to the library today. *(spoken)* Ya-hoo!

Continue in the same fashion with the following verses:

We'll be checking out some books to read today, *(spoken)* Love books!

We'll be checking out some tapes and records, too, *(spoken)* Sing songs!

We'll be seeing puppet shows and movies, too, *(spoken)* Encore!

Yes, we all love going to the library, *(spoken)* Let's go!

OVER THE HIGHWAY AND THROUGH THE TOWN
(Sung to "Over the River and through the Wood")

Over the highway and through the town,
To the library we go;
Mom knows the way,
We go every day,
Because we love it so!

Over the highway and through the town,
Oh, traffic lights please turn.
I've such a list
I can't resist,
So much I want to learn.

RECIPES

The next time you visit your library, why not take in a treat to share with the hard-working librarians? These cookies and bread are appropriate since we are comparing our library to a gold mine. Take in some Golden Nuggets or Apricot Golden Raisin Nut Bread and say, "Thanks!"

GOLDEN NUGGETS
1. Preheat oven to 350 degrees.
2. Blend together $\frac{1}{4}$ cup vegetable oil, $\frac{1}{2}$ cup orange juice concentrate, 1 egg, 2 teaspoons vanilla, and 1 teaspoon orange rind. Pour into a large bowl.
3. Add 2 cups rolled oats, 1 cup wheat germ, and $\frac{1}{4}$ cup chopped nuts.
4. Grate enough carrots to make 1 cup of finely grated carrot and add.
5. Chop 2 slices unsweetened pineapple into small chunks.
6. Mix together well and then drop bite-sized amounts onto a cookie sheet.
7. Bake for 20 minutes.
   Makes approximately 3 dozen cookies.

APRICOT GOLDEN RAISIN NUT BREAD
1. Preheat oven to 350 degrees.
2. Cover $\frac{1}{2}$ cup dried apricots with boiling water and soak for about $\frac{1}{2}$ hour.
3. Squeeze juice from 1 orange and add enough boiling water to make 1 cup; set aside. Save skin.
4. Put drained apricots, cut-up orange skin, and $\frac{1}{2}$ cup golden raisins through food processor; chop lightly.
5. Cream 2 tablespoons margarine and $\frac{1}{2}$ cup sugar; add 1 teaspoon vanilla.
6. Beat in 1 egg. Add fruit and $\frac{1}{2}$ cup chopped nuts.
7. Stir in 2 cups flour, 2 teaspoons baking powder, $\frac{1}{2}$ teaspoon baking soda, and $\frac{1}{4}$ teaspoon salt, alternating with juice.
8. Pour in greased 9-by-5-inch pan and bake for 50-60 minutes.

ACTIVITIES

LIBRARY TREASURE HUNT

To acquaint your child further with your local library, have a book treasure hunt. Explain how books are arranged by author's last name in the Easy Book section and then prepare for a treasure hunt. Locate, ahead of time, a few of your child's favorite books (just to ascertain that they haven't been checked out). Next give clues for each book such as: "I want you to find the book in which we've read about Jenny, Bouncer, and Skog." If that clue isn't enough, go on to another clue: "In this book Bouncer was the leader of the Rough Riding Rowdies." Keep giving clues until your child guesses the book. Then help her with the author's last name and let her begin her search.

When she finds the book, let her check it out to take home.

PERSONALIZED BOOKMARKS

Your child can do this easy and fun project for himself or as gifts for his favorite librarians.

1. Cut a strip of construction paper that measures 2 inches by 8 inches.
2. Place various colors and shapes of colored paper, objects of nature from a spring walk you may take, paper clips, glitter, confetti, or other small flat objects on top of the strip of paper.
3. Take clear contact paper. Cut two pieces slightly bigger than the strip of paper. Peel backing off each strip of contact paper.

4. Place one piece of the contact paper on top of the strip and the other contact paper on the bottom to seal the bookmark. Trim the edges, if necessary.

LIBRARY TRIVIAL PURSUIT

Put together a set of questions that you can ask your child in this mind-game to see just how much he remembers of the books you have been enjoying together. You can make up a game board if you have the desire—even a simple winding path through a forest of books would work. For each question answered correctly he gets to roll a die and move ahead spaces. Some questions might be: Who does Big Anthony work for? What did Petunia think would make her wise? What happened to Curious George when he tried to fly a kite?

THIRD WEEK

Spring Has Returned

Celebrate the fascinating renewal of life as you enjoy the spring activities in this chapter.

READINGS

Big Anthony and the Magic Ring by Tomie de Paola (Harcourt Brace Jovanovich; pb Voyager Books)

When springtime arrives with its blooming flowers, singing birds, and bright sunshine, Big Anthony falls prey to spring fever. "What you need is a little night life," suggests Strega Nona, the village magical Grandma Witch. When Big Anthony follows her suggestions and "borrows" a little of her magic, he gets an unforgettable cure for his spring fever.

Waiting-for-Spring Stories by Bethany Roberts (Harper & Row)

Waiting for spring to arrive can seem endless, but if you are a rabbit, it's not so bad. Rabbits pass the time by telling stories; this book is a collection of seven very special ones.

Three Friends Find Spring by Judy Delton (Crown Publishers)

Rabbit and Squirrel try to cheer up their friend, Duck, who is miserably tired of winter. They bring him all kinds of springtime surprises, but Duck is the one who finally finds the first true sign of spring.

RECITINGS

SPRINGTIME
(Sung to "Do You Know the Muffin Man?")

Do you know that spring is here, spring is here, spring is here?
Do you know that spring is here,
Spring is here to stay?

Yes, I know that spring is here, spring is here, spring is here.
Yes, I know that spring is here,
Spring is here to stay.

I can see that spring is here, the grass is green, the air is clean.
Yes, I can see that spring is here,
Spring is here to stay.

I can hear that spring is here, the birds all sing, and butterflies wing.
Yes, I can see that spring is here,
Spring is here to stay.

I can feel that spring is here, the gentle breeze and no more freeze.
Yes, I can feel that spring is here,
Spring is here to stay.

SPRING FLOWERS
(Sung to "A Tisket, a Tasket")

A tisket, a tasket, a green and yellow basket;
With five spring flowers for my mom, but on the
way I dropped one.
I dropped one, I dropped one, yes on the way I
dropped one.
Now there are four, I'm near the door,
I think I'll knock and shock Mom.

I knocked hard, I knocked hard,
I waited in the front yard.
When Mom arrived I was surprised—
She had eight flowers in her arms!

A dozen, a dozen, twelve flowers makes a dozen.
My four, Mom's eight,
Wow, this is great!
Spring flowers, we just love them!

RECIPES

SPRING FLOWER BREAD

1. Dissolve 1 tablespoon yeast in ¹/₂ cup warm water.
2. Add 1 tablespoon honey and ¹/₄ cup powdered milk.
3. Mix and let stand for 10 minutes.
4. Add 1 egg and 1 cup flour. Beat for 2 minutes.
5. Add ¹/₂ teaspoon salt, 2 tablespoons margarine, and ³/₄ cup flour.
6. Knead. Add additional flour by tablespoons if too sticky to handle.
7. Let the dough rise in oil-covered bowl until it has doubled in bulk (about half an hour).
8. Punch down.
9. Knead in bowl a bit.
10. Divide in half. Cut one half into 4 equal portions and shape into small balls. Cut other half into 2 pieces. Shape one into a larger ball. Cut the other one into 2 more pieces and shape them into 2 smaller balls. You should end up with 6 small balls and 1 slightly larger ball. Place the larger ball in the center of a 9-inch round cake pan and arrange the 6 balls around it, forming a daisy-like shape.
11. Brush all pieces with melted butter.
12. Let rise for 15 minutes.

13. Bake at 400 degrees for 20 minutes.
14. Cool. You'll agree, it's the best "flower" bread you've ever made.

PRETZEL FLOWERS

1. Mix together 1¹/₂ cups warm water, 1 envelope yeast, and 1 tablespoon sugar. Set aside for 5 minutes.
2. Put 1 teaspoon salt and 4 cups flour in a bowl.
3. Add yeast mixture and mix together to form a dough.
4. Shape dough into simple flower shapes. Some suggestions include a tulip, a daisy, or a rose.
5. Beat 1 egg and brush onto the shapes. Sprinkle on coarse salt, if desired.
6. Bake at 425 degrees for 12 minutes.

ACTIVITIES

SPRING WALK

Go for a visual treasure hunt walk to see what changes are taking place now that the weather is warming up. Encourage your child to look for bugs and small creatures appearing, buds on trees and bushes, green coming up through the ground, robins, pussywillows, crocuses, and other early flowers.

APPLE BLOSSOM PICTURES

Have your child use cut-up pieces of sponge to dab pink, green, and white paint on blue construction paper. Once the paint has dried, draw in brown branches.

PAPER FLOWER LEIS

1. Cut 10 2¹/₂-inch flower shapes out of colored construction paper and punch holes in the centers. Anything from a simple circle to a fancy design would be fine for your flower shape.
2. Cut an 18-inch piece of yarn with a long thin noodle tied at one end and the other end taped to make a "needle."
3. Have your child string the flower shapes between more noodle sections to make colorful leis.
4. Tie the yarn ends together when finished.

FOURTH WEEK

April Showers Bring Many Things

To a child an April shower can mean outdoor adventure—a time to grab rainwear and umbrella and splash through every puddle in sight, stomp through every patch of mud around, and dance with every falling raindrop. Or it can mean a day full of warm, cozy inside projects—painting, coloring, reading a favorite book, playing with long-forgotten toys, or baking special goodies.

Whether you choose indoor or outdoor ways to spend your next rainy day (or a few of both), enjoy the activities suggested in this chapter and see what April showers bring you.

READINGS

Peter Spier's Rain by Peter Spier (Doubleday; pb Zephyr Books For Young Readers)

Peter Spier, the master of the wordless picture book, has captured the enchantment of a simple rainstorm with his exceptional artwork. The reader follows a brother and sister's escapades on a fun-filled rainy day.

Bringing the Rain to Kapiti Plain by Verna Aardema (Dial)

The great Kapiti Plain is in trouble for lack of rain. Ki-Pat, the herdsman, helps solve the drought with a little help from an eagle feather. This African tale will remind you of "The House That Jack Built" with its repetition and style.

A Rainbow of My Own by Don Freeman (Penguin Books)

When a little boy sees a rainbow he thinks it is so beautiful he wishes he could catch one for his very own. He imagines many fanciful scenes and discovers a surprise awaiting him in his bedroom.

RECITINGS

MOTHER NATURE'S LULLABY
(Sung to "Brahms Lullaby")

Lullaby, close your eyes,
And just listen intently;
As the rain drops on the rooftop
Let it wash away your cares.
Hear it pour, hear it roar,
Sometimes low, sometimes high,
Let it sing you to sleep,
Mother Nature's lullaby.

SPRING RAIN
(Sung to "Jingle Bells")

Dashing through the rain, on a warm and wet
    spring day,
In puddles I play, laughing all the way.
Slicker on my back, boots to keep me dry,
What fun it is to jump and splash as in this song
    I cry:
Oh, 1-2-3, 1-2-3, spring rain is a friend to me,
Oh, what fun it is to jump in puddles that I see.
Oh, 1-2-3, 1-2-3, spring rain is a friend to me,
Oh, what fun it is to jump in puddles that I see.

RECIPES

RAINBOW COOKIES

These cookies seem rather involved, but they are a treat well worth the extra effort.

1. Mix ^{2}/3 cup margarine, 1 cup sugar, 2 eggs, and 1 teaspoon vanilla until very fluffy.
2. Add 3^1/2 cups flour, 2^1/2 teaspoons baking powder, and ^{1}/2 teaspoon salt.
3. Add 1 tablespoon milk. Mix well and form into a ball of dough.
4. Divide and color a third of the ball of dough pink and a third of it orange. Then divide the last third in half and color one part blue and one green.

Food coloring may be used to attain these colors, but if you are uncomfortable with it, the following are good alternatives. For pink, use ^{1}/2 cup fresh or frozen raspberries that have been pureed. For orange, use the grated rind of half an orange. For blue, use ^{1}/2 cup fresh or frozen blueberries that have been pureed. For green, use 1 tablespoon of creme de menthe or mint extract.

5. Knead in the color well. If using the color alternatives, you may have to add a little extra flour as you knead in the purees.
6. Roll the blue dough into a thick log about 8" long.
7. Roll the green dough into a thick log about 8" long. Flatten slightly and place over the blue log in an arch.
8. Roll the orange dough into a thick log and flatten. Place, in an arch, over the green.
9. Roll the pink dough into a thick log and flatten. Place over the orange.
10. Wrap in plastic wrap and chill at least 2 hours.
11. Preheat oven to 400 degrees.
12. Slice dough rolls into ^{1}/4-inch pieces, cutting all the way through all the "logs" so that each resulting cookie has four colors.
12. Place on ungreased cookie sheet and bake for 9 minutes.

Makes approximately 2 dozen cookies.

RAINBOW SALAD

This delicious coleslaw is as colorful as a rainbow.

1. Chop ^{1}/2 small head of purple cabbage and ^{1}/2 small head of green cabbage as for coleslaw.
2. Add 2 medium carrots, shredded.
3. Drain 1 (8-ounce) can pineapple tidbits, reserving 3 tablespoons of the juice.
4. Add 2 Red Delicious apples, chopped with the skin, to the pineapple and juice. Mix all ingredients together.

Dressing: Mix together ^{1}/2 cup mayonnaise, ^{1}/2 cup plain yogurt, 1 tablespoon lemon juice, 1 tablespoon honey, ^{1}/2 teaspoon salt, ^{1}/2 teaspoon celery seed, and 1 teaspoon dill seed. Pour over salad and toss.

ACTIVITIES

OUTDOOR RAIN FUN

A rainy day can offer a wonderful outdoor playtime. Once dressed in boots, raincoat, and rainhat, a child need know no limits. Puddles, mud, and bike-riding through the rain are all appealing options—as long as there are warm, dry clothes to change into afterward. Let your child have fun splashing through as much rain as she'd like.

INDOOR RAIN FUN

Outline pretend puddles with chalk or masking tape on the floor. Take turns running around and over and through the puddles to the sound of music or the clapping of hands. When the music or hand-clapping stops (controlled by you) whoever is in the puddle or is closest to it loses—and has to go home to put on dry clothes. Repeat as many times as you'd like.

MAKE A HOMEMADE RAINBOW

On a piece of white paper draw six arcs for a rainbow. Use a red, orange, yellow, green, blue, and violet crayon to mark off each section. Cut or tear out pictures from magazines that have patches of the rainbow colors.

Have your child glue the magazine picture pieces onto the appropriate colored arc, trying to fill each section in with as much of that particular color as possible. When he finishes he'll have a rainbow collage to display.

CHAPTER FIVE

MAY

A Month to Celebrate Mothers

The child in every one of us directs his attention to mothers during the month of May. Loving thoughts, special gifts, and kind deeds are all given to dear Mom on the second Sunday in May in celebration of Mother's Day.

And another mother comes into full bloom during this month—Mother Nature. She now brings more hours of sunlight to provide more play time outdoors and more growing time for blossoming plants.

Celebrate this time of year with the mothers who bring beauty and love into your child's life as you enjoy some of the activities offered in this chapter.

FIRST WEEK

THANKS, DAYLIGHT SAVINGS TIME

Daylight Savings Time was initiated back in 1918 to help conserve fuel by extending daylight by one extra hour. That extra hour of daylight may be making conservation easier, but it has made something else harder—children's bedtime. As if bedtime weren't difficult enough already, now with Daylight Savings Time, most children are expected to go to bed when it is still light outside. By the end of the day, and with the bedtime struggles that sometimes ensue, even the most patient parent has the tendency to "lose it"! However, many times tough situations can be avoided with a little planning ahead and humor. Consider some of the suggestions below and make bedtime more pleasant and easy for all.

READINGS

Bedtime for Frances by Russell Hoban (Harper & Row)

Frances, the badger, doesn't want to go to bed, and she tries every stalling trick ever tried, from asking for one more kiss to one more glass of milk. Her parents handle her requests and fears patiently, lovingly, and firmly.

Moonlight by Jan Ormerod (Lothrop, Lee & Shepard Books)

This wordless picture book takes a little girl through all of her nightly bedtime rituals from bathtime to story time to the last extra kiss. But she still isn't quite ready to sleep. The interesting twist at the end of the book will delight all who read it.

The Summer Night by Charlotte Zolotow (Harper & Row)

When Daddy puts his little girl to bed one summer night he can see her eyes are as bright as the stars. She is not sleepy enough for bed. So he enjoys one thing after another with her—from a story to a song to a moonlit walk—until she finally has a dreamy look in her eyes. This is a soft, gentle bedtime story.

RECITINGS

TWINKLE, TWINKLE, BEDTIME STAR
(Sung to "Twinkle, Twinkle, Little Star")

Twinkle, twinkle, bedtime star,
How I wonder where you are,
In winter when I go to bed,
You shine down on my sleepy head.

But now that summertime is here,
Bedtime comes and you're not there,
It's so hard to say good night
When it's not dark, but still so light.

Twinkle, twinkle, bedtime star,
How I wonder where you are.

THREE SLEEPYHEADS
(Sung to "Three Blind Mice")

Three sleepyheads,
Three sleepyheads,
See how they yawn,
See how they yawn,
But when it's bedtime excuses come,
More water, more hugs, just another one,
More stories, more songs when the day is done,
For three sleepyheads.

RECIPES

ACTIVITIES

FUN FORTUNE COOKIES

Rather than a bedtime snack (which is not recommended if your child has eaten a good dinner), these cookies can be a dessert treat. Instead of writing fortunes or riddles, write bedtime excuses on strips of paper and use them as Bedtime Stallers (see project below).

1. Combine 1/3 cup flour, 1 1/2 tablespoons brown sugar, a dash of salt, and 1 1/2 tablespoons cornstarch.
2. Mix 2 tablespoons oil and 1 egg white, beaten stiff. Add to the flour mix.
3. Add 4 tablespoons water and 1/2 teaspoon vanilla. Mix well.
4. Pour 1 heaping tablespoon of batter on a non-stick skillet, using medium heat. Spread into a 3-inch circle.
5. Cook 4 minutes until brown. Turn and cook 2 minutes on other side.
6. Remove from pan. Place bedtime excuse strip on circle. Use oven mitt to fold circle in half, pressing firmly. Bend folded side over rim of a cup.
7. Cool in an empty egg carton.
8. Crisp cookies in a 350-degree oven for 10 minutes.
   Makes 8 cookies.

MINI-COFFEECAKES

These make great little snacks to leave out in the morning. (See Morning Surprises below.)

1. Preheat oven to 350 degrees.
2. Beat 1/2 cup oil, 2 eggs, and 1/3 cup sugar together.
3. Add 1 cup plain yogurt and 1 1/2 teaspoons vanilla.
4. Add 1/2 cup whole wheat flour, 1/2 cup white flour, 1/2 cup wheat germ, 1/2 teaspoon baking powder, 1 teaspoon baking soda, and 1/2 teaspoon cinnamon.
5. Beat and pour half of the batter into greased muffin tins. Sprinkle each muffin with a combination of chopped walnuts, cinnamon, and sugar. Then pour the rest of the batter on top of each muffin.
6. Bake for 25 minutes.

BEDTIME STALLERS

First brainstorm with your child to come up with all the excuses he usually uses when he wants to postpone bedtime. Once you have several, explain the following new plan. Each night he can choose one of the stallers to use at bedtime. You can either write them out on special cards or make them the strips that go into your fortune cookies (see above). At a time that is mutually agreed upon, he may pick his staller for the night, which will be the only excuse you will give in to for that evening.

To make the bedtime excuses as cards:

Take poster board or index cards and write the excuses, one on each, with a felt-tipped pen. You may also add a simple drawing on each for the non-readers. Laminate them with clear contact paper and put them in a box. They may be selected at random or used in rotation. Some suggestions for excuses: "one more drink of water" (draw a glass), "one more kiss" (draw lips), "one more story" (draw a book), "one more lullaby" (draw musical notes), "need my teddy bear" or other stuffed animal (draw animal), or "need to go to the bathroom" (draw a toilet).

BEDTIME EXCUSES

MORNING SURPRISE

Sometimes children don't want the day to be over because they're afraid they will miss out on something. A promise of a morning surprise may be just the incentive to encourage bedtime cooperation.

For a child who cooperates at bedtime there will be a surprise on the kitchen table (or other designated place) in the morning. Suggestions: fruit or other simple breakfast snacks (Mini-Coffeecakes), coloring books, books to read, or simple art projects. Be sure to leave things that don't need explanations so that if she gets up before you do, you may be able to get a few extra minutes of sleep yourself!

MORNING PUZZLE PROJECT

Cut out some colorful and interesting pictures from magazines and glue them to poster board. Cover them with clear contact paper. Then cut it into puzzle pieces, letting your child's age and ability determine the size and number of pieces. Leave this puzzle out on the table for her to do in the morning when she gets up.

SECOND WEEK

Treating Mom on Mother's Day

If you are a mom, please put a bookmark here, close the book up, and give it to someone in your family who can read the next few pages. Read no further for now.

If you are a dad, a son, a daughter, another relative, or a very close friend who loves Mom, this section is important for you to read.

Mom is a very dear person in your life. What makes her such a good buddy to you? Does she bake brownies for you, push you on your swing, take you to the park, sing lullabies to you at bedtime, read books to you, or hug you when you need it the most? Undoubtedly you have your own reasons for why you love your mom so much. On Mother's Day, the second Sunday of May, share your reasons with her. Let Mom know just how you feel. Do a few things that day to show your appreciation. Most likely you've given it some thought already, but listed below are some suggestions of a few easy and memorable things to do.

READINGS

Happy Mother's Day by Steven Kroll (Holiday House)

Every mom wants to be treated like a queen on Mother's Day, and in this book she is. Through simple yet meaningful acts and inexpensive or handmade gifts, this family treats their mom to a tender and unforgettable Mother's Day.

The Mother's Day Mice by Eve Bunting (Clarion Books)

Big, Middle, and Little Mouse wake up very early on Mother's Day and set out to get gifts for their mom. Big selects a fluffy white wish flower; Middle chooses a red ripe strawberry; but Cat is guarding Little's choice of a spray of honeysuckle. Little is disappointed at first, but manages to come up with an even better gift of love for his mom.

Hooray for Mother's Day! by Marjorie Weinman Sharmat (Holiday House)

Alaric Chicken wants to find the perfect gift for his mother. But this is not an easy task. Every gift he inspects has something terribly wrong with it. Slippers might make his mother fall, chocolate might give her cavities. Everything seems hopeless. But Alaric does find the perfect gift and the reader will be surprised at what it is.

RECITINGS

HAPPY MOTHER'S DAY TO YOU
(Sung to "Happy Birthday")

Happy Mother's Day to you,
Happy Mother's Day to you,
I've got some surprises
To celebrate with you.

The very first treat
Is something to eat—
I'm serving you breakfast,
Fruit, eggs, toast, and tea.

The flowers on the tray
I picked fresh today;
The cards and the gifts
I made yesterday.

Then after this we'll do
What you want to do;
I love you, dear Mommy,
Happy Mother's Day to you.

WHAT A LADY
(Sung to "London Bridge")

Mommy's love spreads all around,
All around, all around.
Mommy's love spreads all around—
What a lady.

When she hugs me tight, I feel all right,
Feel all right, feel all right.
When she hugs me tight, I feel all right—
What a lady.

We sing and play the whole day through,
The whole day through, the whole day through.
We sing and play the whole day through—
What a lady.

I love her so and that is true,
That is true, that is true.
I love her so and that is true—
What a lady.

MOTHER'S DAY BREAKFAST IN BED

Breakfast in bed is an excellent way to start Mom's special day. Prepare a nutritious and elegant breakfast, arrange it on a tray along with a flower in a vase, and when she awakens on Mother's Day morning, give her the treat of a lifetime. The three recipes offered below make tasty breakfast choices.

RECIPES

WAKE-UP JUICE
Blend together $1/3$ cup nonfat dry milk, a 6-ounce can frozen orange-pineapple juice concentrate, 1 cup water, and $1/2$ cup crushed ice to make a super drink. Serve it in a pretty champagne or wine glass with a whole strawberry floating on top.

EGG-IN-A-HEART BASKET
1. Put a small dab of margarine in a frying pan. Turn the burner on to medium heat and let the margarine melt.
2. Take one piece of bread and cut out a heart shape in the middle of the bread. (Use a cookie-cutter or even do it freehand with a knife.)
3. Put the bread in the pan. Crack an egg inside the heart-shaped cut-out and allow it to cook.
4. When one side is cooked, flip the treat to the other side and finish frying. When the egg is

cooked to your mom's general liking, take it out of the pan, put the heart cut-out on top, and place it all on a plate.

"YOU ARE MY SUNSHINE" SALAD
1. Put 1 slice of pineapple on a dish.
2. Put 1 tablespoon of Mom's favorite flavored yogurt in the middle.
3. Put almonds along the outside of the pineapple ring to look like sun rays.

ACTIVITIES

MOTHER'S DAY CARD
This card will be a booklet with the same number of pages as there are children in your family. Each child will do one page of the booklet. Decide what shape you want the pages to be—heart-shaped, circular, square, or whatever other shape you desire—cut the number of pages you need, and hand one to each child. Each of you can either draw a picture or glue on a photograph of Mom doing something special with you. Write on either the front or back page, "We all love you, Mom," and then each of you sign your name.

CRUMB SCRAPER/CATCHER
Often family meals leave crumbs on the table. Help Mom out by making and using a crumb scraper/catcher.

1. Take two stiff paper plates. Decorate both plates as you wish, front and back, either with crayons, paint, or felt markers, or by gluing on materials.
2. Cut one of the plates in half. Align one half with the other whole plate, back side facing out so that it makes a little pocket. Staple them together. This is the catcher. You may want to write "Catcher" in bold letters on the plate.
3. Use the other half as the scraper. You may wish to write "Scraper" in bold letters on it.

"PROMISES, PROMISES"
1. Take 10 index cards.
2. Write on each one a promise your mom can claim as a special and personal gift.
3. Some promises might be: "I will make my own bed," "I will set the table," "I will clear the table," "I will put my toys away without being asked," "I will hang up my clothes," "I will fold laundry."
4. Decorate with stickers or little drawings.

THIRD WEEK

Dandelion Delight

When you can take just one glance out the window to confirm that it is dandelion season, it is the right time for this section. Whether your yard is speckled with yellow dots or blanketed with white fluff, dandelions are more than likely moving into your neighborhood for the summer. As adults, we'd love to rid our lawns of these tough weeds. But children view dandelions in a completely different light. Believe it or not, these nasty weeds can provide all kinds of fun and wishful excitement for our carefree children. Read on to discover the delight of dandelions.

READINGS

Barney Bipple's Magic Dandelions by Carol Chapman (E.P. Dutton)

When Barney Bipple is given three magic dandelions from his neighbor, Minerva Merkle, he knows exactly what to wish for. But he learns that sometimes wishes don't turn out to be exactly what one expects.

The Tiny Seed by Eric Carle (Crowell)

The life cycle of a flowering plant is beautifully told in this colorful book. With the help of autumn's strong winds, winter's cold white blanket, spring's rain, and summer's nurturing sun the tiny seed survives and thrives.

Dandelions by Kathleen Pohl (Raintree Publishers)

This "nature close-up" book not only tells more than you can imagine about the dandelion but also features photographs of dandelions in their varied forms. A very accurate, scientific, and enjoyable book.

RECITINGS

DANDELION MAGIC
(Sung to "Did You Ever See a Lassie?")

Did you ever see a magic show,
A magic show, a magic show—
Did you ever see a magic show,
With a magician and his hat?

He puts in a chick,
Says a chant, waves his stick;
Then a bunny pops his head out—
I just love that trick!
And did you ever see a magic show,
A magic show, a magic show—
Did you ever see a magic show
Out on your front lawn?

One day all you see
Is green grass, tree to tree—
Then one day yellow takes over,
Almost magically!

I'M A LITTLE GENIE
(Sung to "I'm a Little Teapot")

I'm a little genie
In this vase,
Rub it three times
And I'll show my face.
If you have a wish
Just tell me true,
And then I'll see what I can do.

RECIPES

MAGIC RAISINS

1. Wash and dry 2 cups of fresh grapes.
2. Place grapes in a dish in a sunny, warm place.
3. When grapes have dried into raisins, make Magic Raisins.
(As this takes up to 15 days, you may wish to skip steps 1-3 and use store-bought raisins.)
4. Pour any sparkling water, such as Perrier, club soda, seltzer, or lemon soda, into a tall, clear glass. Add 4 to 6 raisins. Watch carefully. Raisins will sink to the bottom, then slowly rise to the top. They will continue to jump up and down, as if by magic, for several minutes.
5. Wait until all the raisins settle to the bottom of the glass, then drink the soda. Get a spoon, scoop out the raisins, and eat them.

MAGIC JELL-O

1. Prepare a package of fruit-flavored Jell-O according to the directions. Or make some gelatin with Knox flavored gelatin. (To 1 envelope of Knox gelatin, add 1 cup of boiling juice and 1 cup of cool juice, in whatever flavors you choose.)
2. Prepare the Jell-O in a clear bowl, if possible.

3. When the solution is cool, but not hard, add some or all of the following: any kind of berry—like blueberries, raspberries, strawberries, or blackberries; sliced bananas; sliced peaches; grated coconut; grated carrots; chopped walnuts; raisins; other dried fruit; crushed pineapple.
4. Some of the things will "magically" sink and others will float. Talk about the principles of sinking and floating.
5. Chill the Jell-O and see the layers of items.

ACTIVITIES

DANDELION WALK

Take a walk and study the various dandelions outside. Some suggestions of what you and your child can do are: Pick a yellow one and a white puffy one. Notice similarities and differences in the two stages. Try to dig one up, root and all. Try to count all the yellow ones you can see in a particular area. Try to count the white ones. Notice where the most dandelions are growing—sunny or shaded areas.

MAGIC PICTURES

Take two sheets of paper and paper-clip them together. Place any flat object, such as a coin, paper clip, comb, or string, between them. Do all of this ahead of time so that your child doesn't see.

Have your child take a peeled crayon and, with the flat side of the crayon, color the paper. The objects will appear just like magic!

DANDELION DESIGNS

Pick some dandelions that are white and fuzzy and bring them inside. Blow the seedlings on glue-spotted paper. See what patterns emerge.

DANDELION STRAWS

The stalk of a dandelion is hollow. Break off the flower and use the stalk to blow bubbles by dipping one end in bubble solution and blowing through the other end.

FOURTH WEEK

How Does Your Garden Grow?

"Mary, Mary, quite contrary,
How does your garden grow?"
"With silver bells, and cockle shells,
And pretty maids all in a row."

Your name may not be Mary, and you probably have never planted a garden with silver bells and cockle shells and pretty maids all in a row. But have you ever planted something? Can you remember the anticipation as you waited, the excitement as you watched, and the pride as you harvested the fruit of your labor? Whether it was a glass jar of bean sprouts, a colorful spread of spring bulbs, or a full-scale outdoor vegetable garden, the emotional involvement was the same. Help your child experience these feelings as you explore together some of the varied gardening activities in this chapter.

READINGS

The Giant Vegetable Garden by Nadine Westcott (Atlantic Monthly Press; pb Little Brown & Co.)

When the Mayor of Peapack involves his town in a county fair's vegetable contest, the whole town gets greedy for the prize money. Bigger means better in their minds, so the vegetables are grown to exaggerated sizes. But when the contest is over, what can be done with vegetables the size of houses? This amusing storyline is only outdone by the hysterical illustrations that depict the silliness of the situation.

Your First Garden Book by Marc Brown (Atlantic Monthly Press; pb Little Brown & Co.)

You will get numerous ideas for every kind of gardening possible in this book. From planting potatoes in a bucket indoors to planting flowers in the sidewalk cracks, you'll find ideas to satisfy the gardener in us all.

How to Grow a Jelly Glass Farm by Kathy Mandry (Pantheon Books)

If you would like to try your green thumb at growing some easy and exciting indoor plants, this is a great book for you. You'll learn how to grow an alligator, a pot of sunshine, a prickly mountain, and twelve other fun plants all from pits, seeds, and other leftover parts of foods you eat.

RECITINGS

THE GARDENER PLANTS THE SEEDS
(Sung to "The Farmer in the Dell")

The gardener plants the seeds,
The gardener plants the seeds.
Heigh-o the derry-o,
The gardener plants the seeds.

The rain waters the seeds, *etc.*
The sun warms the seeds, *etc.*
The seeds grow into plants, *etc.*
The plants produce some fruit, *etc.*
The gardener picks the fruit, *etc.*
The gardener eats some fruit, *etc.*
The gardener saves the seeds, *etc.*
The gardener plants the seeds, *etc.*

RAIN, RAIN, COME TODAY
(Sung to "Rain, Rain")

Rain, rain, come today,
On this gentle day in May.
I planted seeds yesterday,
Please come water them today.

SPROUTS, SPROUTS, SPROUTS!

Most children love growing sprouts because they grow quickly and are fun to watch. Children can grow sprouts in glass jars or in small zip-lock plastic bags. Glass jars should be covered with a square of cheesecloth or nylon stocking and secured with a rubber band. If you choose to use small plastic bags, stick 10 or so holes in the bottom of the bag with a large needle. Be sure that some holes are right on the bottom crease so that the water will drain well from the bag.

Have your child fill his jar or bag ⅛ to ¼ full with sprout seeds. Fill the jar with warm water. Soak the seeds overnight. Have your child drain the seeds well and place them in a light place, but not in direct sunlight. For the next 3 to 4 days have your child rinse and drain the seeds daily. Place sprouts in direct sunlight on the last day and they will green up more. Store sprouts in the refrigerator. They should stay fresh for 10 to 14 days.

Some fun things to do with sprouts:

Add them to sandwiches—peanut butter and sprouts, cream cheese and sprouts, tuna fish and sprouts, egg salad and sprouts, toasted cheese and sprouts.

Make open-faced sandwiches—cut the bread in a circle, then decorate as a person, using the sprouts for hair and other features.

Make a salad using all kinds of fresh vegetables and sprouts.

As a snack or appetizer—toast English muffins, spread on peanut butter, and top with sprouts. Cut in fours and serve (or put sprouts on top of the toasted English muffin and place a slice of cheese over them, then melt under the broiler).

Top cheese and crackers or peanut butter and crackers with piles of sprouts.

Add your own creative cookery ideas to the list.

RECIPES

VEGGIE DIP

This luscious dip is a great appetizer or snack when served with fresh vegetables (especially from your own garden!).

1. Thaw 1 10-ounce package of frozen chopped spinach and drain well until barely moist.
2. Combine it with ½ cup mayonnaise, ½ cup sour cream, 1 cup plain yogurt, 1 8-ounce can water chestnuts, chopped, and 1 package vegetable soup mix.
3. Stir well. Cover and chill several hours.

CHUNKY VEGETABLE DIP

Another delicious dip to use with your home-grown vegetables.

1. Place into a blender or food processor: 6 cherry tomatoes, 1 medium pepper cut into chunks, ½ cup plain yogurt, ½ cup cottage cheese, ½ teaspoon dill, ½ teaspoon celery seed, and a pinch of salt. Process until chunky and well-blended.
2. Scrape all the dip into a bowl and serve with cut-up raw vegetables.

ACTIVITIES

EGGSHELL GARDEN

Indoor gardening or beginning seeds indoors can be exciting, for within just a few days or weeks of the original planting of the seeds, little sprouts can be seen.

1. Crack an egg and save the larger half of the shell.
2. Fill the shell with soil (better when mixed with a little vermiculite, available at nurseries or department stores).
3. Have your child plant 3 or 4 seeds in the soil and water them.

4. Repeat this process with as many eggshells as you'd like, using as many different kinds of seeds as you'd like. (Radish seeds are perhaps the easiest to grow.)
5. Keep the various shells in an egg carton bottom and you have an eggshell garden.
6. Put the garden in a sunny spot and water soil to keep evenly damp.
7. As the seedlings grow you will want to thin them out to only one per eggshell. If hardy enough, they can be planted outdoors after the danger of frost has passed.

The same type of activity is offered through pre-packaged kits available in most department stores or nurseries. (One brand name is Sow'n'Gro.)

TOPS GARDEN

In this gardening experiment your child will learn that a plant doesn't always need soil to grow.

Cut off the tops of turnips, carrots, pineapples, or beets. Have your child place them each in a shallow dish with the cut side facing down in the water. In a few days greens will start to grow. Eventually you can transplant the plant to the soil.

GARDENING EXPERIMENT

Plants naturally turn toward light. To prove this, ask your child to place several plants on a window ledge and watch them bend toward the sunlight. She can turn them after several days and watch their activity. Have her put one plant in a dark closet for three days, while she leaves another plant on the window ledge. Compare the differences with her.

MAPPING OUT YOUR GARDEN

Whether you plan to plant a real garden this year or not, this can be a fun activity. Discuss the various plants your child wants to grow—which ones are sensible for his own situation—and draw a little sketch of what his garden will look like. Perhaps it will be 5 by 5 feet, and he'll grow radishes, lettuce, carrots, beans, and tomatoes. Draw a 5-inch square. Divide it into 5 rows, then draw in the 5 different vegetables he'll raise. If this is a pretend activity, let your child be creative, envisioning all the watermelons and pumpkins he'd like!

FIFTH WEEK

Memorial Day Parade Fun

To adults, Memorial Day is a day set aside to honor all the war dead. We remember those brave souls who died for our country and we decorate their graves. But to children, Memorial Day is much simpler: it is a day of parades—parades blaring with melodic marching bands; parades beaming with pride as children affiliated with various youth organizations try to keep in step; parades proudly displaying their town's glistening fire engines; and parades hosting vendors of colorful balloons and yummy treats. Memorial Day is now celebrated on the last Monday in May. Check your local newspaper for your town parade's starting time and enjoy some of the pre-parade activities that follow.

READINGS

Parade by Donald Crews (Greenwillow)

Anticipation builds in this book as the crowd gathers and awaits the parade. Once it arrives, it comes complete with flying flags, a strutting drum major who leads the marching band, floats, baton twirlers, antique bicycles, cars, and fire engines. Donald Crews's simple artwork and his use of carefully selected phrases make this book a winner with children, for they can virtually read this book by themselves.

Melissa on Parade by Tom Reed (Bradbury Press)

Melissa loves parades. Every time she and her two dogs go to one she tries to get involved in it. But she is never allowed to take part. Then one day she sees something happening that demands not only her attention but the help of the paraders, too. Melissa gets very involved and saves the day.

The Parade by Kjell Ringi (Franklin Watts, Inc.)

A parade twenty strong marches on, stopping for nothing that crosses its path. Up and over a tall giraffe, up and down a rocky cliff—nothing stops the marchers until they reach a small thing of beauty that they just can't pass by. This rhyming story shows the powers of love and beauty.

RECITINGS

THERE WAS ONE IN THE BAND
(Sung to "Roll Over")

There was one in the band,
But he had a plan
For others, for others.
So he held out his hand
For another one,
And, . . .

There were two in the band,
But they had a plan
For others, for others.
So they held out their hands
For another one,
And, . . .

Continue up to nine and then end with:
There were ten in the band
And they sounded so GRAND!

THE BANDS IN THE PARADE
(Sung to "The Wheels of the Bus")

The bands in the parade march left and right,
Left and right, left and right.

The bands in the parade march left and right,
All through the town.

The floats in the parade move gracefully, *etc.*

The trucks in the parade honk their loud horns, *etc.*

The horses in the parade go clippety-clop, *etc.*

The mayor in the parade waves to the crowd, *etc.*

The clowns in the parade make everyone laugh, *etc.*

Add any other verses you and your child can make up.

PARADE MUSIC

The book Parade *lends itself to discussing the various types of musical instruments found in a band. The book shows and labels many of them. If your child is interested in musical instruments, this is a great time to delve a little deeper—get several more books from the library and/or a recording or two that plays the various sounds of different instruments. Summertime outdoor concerts might be of interest at this age, as well.*

RECIPES

Try both of these fun recipes for quick-energy, easy-to-carry munchies to take with you to the parade.

APPLE SANDWICH

Core an apple and fill it with a mixture of 1 tablespoon peanut butter, 1 teaspoon wheat germ, and 1 teaspoon coconut. Great for taking to a parade.

STRINGY SNACK

1. Set out in individual bowls some or all of the following: dried apples, apricots, dried pineapple, prunes, figs, raisins, popcorn, Cheerios, pretzels.
2. Pick favorite ingredients and set out in a pattern.
3. Use a large, blunt needle and knotted thread to string the food.
4. Use scissors and cut off the needle. Knot the ends of the string and wear as a necklace. Nibble as needed.

ACTIVITIES

FOLLOW THE LEADER

Choose who will be the leader, then have the other players line up directly behind the leader. Everyone has to copy the leader's motions. Then a new leader is picked. Some suggested motions: jump up and down, bounce a ball and walk, skip, wave arms up and down, do somersaults, hop on one foot, bend at the waist, and touch toes.

Once you have successfully established a good follow-the-leader format, play again, this time pretending to be a band. The leader will be the drum major leading her band.

MAKING YOUR OWN BAND

Almost anything can be used to improvise your own musical instruments. Help your children make some or all of the following and take turns playing the various instruments when they "march" in their next parade.

Coffee Can Drum

Take a coffee can or round carton with a tight-fitting lid, attach a string to it so that it can be carried over the child's shoulder (supervise carefully to be sure he doesn't wind the string by accident around his neck), and use two sticks or wooden spoons as the drumsticks.

Stringed Instruments

Cut a hole in the cover of a shoebox. Tape the cover to the box so it doesn't fall off. Stretch rubber bands over the box and plunk away with your fingers.

Cymbals

Clang pot covers together.

Shakers

Put dry macaroni or beans in an oatmeal cylinder, tape securely, and shake.

Fife

Take an empty paper towel cardboard roll. Punch five small holes in it, using the tip of a pencil. Cover one end with waxed paper and secure it with tape. When you hum into it, the sound is amplified. By covering the holes with your fingers, you can produce different notes.

Harmonicas

Blow on combs covered with wax paper.

Sandpaper Blocks

Take two wooden blocks and either glue or tack sandpaper to them. When they are rubbed together in time to the music, the sandpaper produces a shuffling sound.

MARCHING PRACTICE

The familiar chant of the armed forces, "Left—left—left—right—left," is an interesting way to practice marching as well as distinguishing left from right.

Begin marching in place, mark time as it is called, and coordinate your left foot with your child's left foot. You may wish to beat on a drum or clap your hands to keep a beat. Once your child and you are synchronized, begin marching in various directions and patterns. Move to the left; turn to the right; call the directions out clearly and try to stay together. Once you get really good at it, march in a pattern that will make a certain shape, either a square, a rectangle, or a triangle, and see if your child can figure out what you made.

CHAPTER SIX

JUNE
A Month to Relish Summer Freedoms

*School dismisses for the summer recess during the month of
June, setting children free to enjoy some time off.
Now there is time to sleep in, to indulge in a late morning
pancake feast, or to plan and partake of a fun-filled
picnic. Now there is time to go fishing with Daddy or spend
"his" day in another relaxed way he would like.*

*Now there is time to spend a lazy
summer afternoon down at a pond
watching and playing with the frogs.
Next to a child's birthday month,
June is perhaps her favorite month of
the year, for it heralds the freshness
and beauty of the summer season.
Welcome summertime with your
child with some of the fun activities
offered in this chapter.*

FIRST WEEK

Picture Perfect for a Picnic

It is a picture-perfect day, a meteorologist's dream come true: 75 degrees, not a cloud in the sky, low humidity, with an ever-so-gentle breeze. It is the kind of day that almost demands your postponing all indoor obligations to get outside to soak in some of nature's beauty.

READINGS

The Bears' Picnic by Stan and Jan Berenstain (Beginner)

When Father Bear invites his family to go on a picnic, everyone is all smiles until they try to find a perfect picnicking spot. After escaping mosquitoes, a thunderstorm, crowds of other picnickers, and a low-flying jet (to name just a few of the obstacles), the bear family finally locates the best spot and wearily sits down to eat.

This book, as well as many other of the Berenstain Bears books, comes with a tape that makes it a good listening activity, read-along book, and traveling companion for the car.

The Teddy Bears' Picnic by Jimmy Kennedy (Green Tiger Press)

The teddy bears have a picnic for every bear who has been good. There are goodies to eat and games to play and all kinds of festivities. An accompanying record tucked in the back of the book helps to make this story unforgettable.

Picnic by Emily Arnold McCully (Harper & Row)

A large family of mice nearly has a disaster on a picnic, but all ends happily in this tender, wordless picture book.

RECITINGS

LET'S GO ON A PICNIC
(Sung to "Row, Row, Row Your Boat")

Let's go on a picnic—
What a special treat!
What are some of the yummy things
We can bring to eat?

Let's bring sandwiches,
Juice and cookies, too;
Apples, oranges, grapes, and nuts
Are great for me and you.

Add your own verses for the items you are going to bring.

OUR PICNIC
Look out the window—
The sun shines so bright.
Let's go on a picnic—
We'll stay until the night.

First we must get ready;
There is so much to bring—
Food, drinks, toys and games,
Let's not forget a thing.

Peanut butter sandwiches,
So tasty and such fun;
Peanut butter shakes and squares
To enjoy out in the sun.

We'll save some leftovers for the ants.
Why not? They're hungry, too.
We can watch and see how much
They work and what they do.

Lie back beneath the clear blue sky.
This truly is a day
To have a super dazzling time
Picnicking this way.

RECIPES

HOMEMADE PEANUT BUTTER

Take one cup of peanuts (raw or roasted). Put them in a blender or food processor. Blend until it is the consistency that you like. To make it more spreadable, you may wish to add 1 tablespoon of oil. You may also wish to add a pinch of salt and/or sugar, but it really tastes great without them.

PEANUT BUTTER SQUARES

1. Preheat oven to 375 degrees.
2. Cream together ½ cup margarine, ½ cup peanut butter, ½ cup firmly packed brown sugar, and 1 egg.
3. Stir in 2 tablespoons water, 1¼ cups flour, ¾ teaspoon baking soda, ½ teaspoon baking powder, and ¼ teaspoon salt.
4. Fold in ½ cup of semisweet chocolate morsels.
5. Spread in greased 13-by-9-by-2-inch baking pan. Bake for 20 minutes. Cool and cut.

PEANUT BUTTER PICNIC

If your child loves peanut butter as so many children do, focus your picnic on peanut butter.

Begin with your own homemade peanut butter, as mentioned above, and then use it in some of the following picnic treats:

■ *Peanut butter sandwiches, topped with any or all of the following: jelly, jam, bananas, apple slices, applesauce, sprouts, grated carrots, chopped celery, granola, sunflower seeds, other nuts, coconut, banana chips, raisins.*

■ *Celery logs—Mix equal portions of grated carrots, peanut butter, and spoon-sized shredded wheat (smashed) and press mixture into celery sticks.*

■ *Apple and peanut butter—Cut a small apple in half. Scoop out the seeds and fill the holes with peanut butter.*

■ *Peanut butter shake—Blend together 1 cup milk, 1 ripe banana, and 1 tablespoon of peanut butter. Chill and put in a Thermos.*

Try to have everyone wear tan or brown "peanut butter" clothes.

Instead of a tablecloth to spread out, bring along a large sheet of butcher paper and crayons. Decorate the butcher paper as a huge peanut butter sandwich. The tan paper can be the bread, and use crayons to draw in the peanut butter and whatever else you have in your sandwiches.

After eating, enjoy a special peanut treasure hunt with shelled peanuts that you've packed and try doing some of the activities mentioned below.

ACTIVITIES

ANT LEFTOVERS

After you have finished eating, rather than throw the crumbs away, conduct a live science experiment and feed the ants. Find a mound of sand or dirt where ants are living. Feed them some tiny crumbs of bread or other leftovers and watch what happens. Where do they go? How do they carry the food? See how much you can both learn just from careful observation.

NATURE SCULPTURES

Together, gather some good-looking twigs and sticks (dead ones only), acorns, pine needles, pebbles, and other pieces of nature. Plan and sculpt a design. Tape or tie the wood pieces together to hold them in place. Squeeze glue to join the sticks together permanently. When they are firmly together, remove the tape or string from the sculpture.

Plan ahead for this project—bring tape and glue with you on your picnic.

CLOUD WATCHING

Lie down with your child and gaze up at the clouds. Imagine they are creatures or painted scenes or people or monsters. Watch them as they pass by.

SECOND WEEK

Happy Daddy's Day

Gone are the days when Father was the sole breadwinner and the stern disciplinarian. Today's father is much more complex. He is more involved in the birth process, child-rearing, and even the household chores than yesteryear's father. It is not unusual to see dads in grocery stores, at school conferences, or out strolling the baby. And the real beauty of it is that Dad is loving every minute of it! Sure, parenthood is difficult and certainly has its exhausting moments, but dads are finally feeling freer to enjoy their children as they take an active part in raising them.

The second Sunday in June is Father's Day, a national holiday that became official when President Richard Nixon signed a law in 1972. Take time now to plan something special for the man who adds a marvelous dimension to your family's life. Below are some suggestions of how to help your child show Daddy the love and appreciation he deserves.

Just Like Daddy by Frank Asch (Prentice-Hall)

Little Bear spends an entire day doing everything just like Daddy, until they go fishing. The clever twist at the end of this story will bring a smile to all who read it.

RECITINGS

MY BEST PLAYMATE
(Sung to "Pop Goes the Weasel")

All around our great big house,
My daddy chases me.
He gets so close,
Then suddenly,
Tag! I am it.

All around our great big house,
I hide in secret places.
Daddy tries to find me and then,
Pop! I find him.

I love to play so many games
With Daddy all the time.
He's the best playmate of all,
And I love him.

READINGS

Matthew and his Dad by Arlene Alda (Simon & Schuster)

This story about a real child's love, need, and admiration for his dad contains photographs and a partly fictional storyline.

Just Me and My Dad by Mercer Mayer (Western Publishing Co)

When Little Monster and his dad go camping together, Little Monster does all he can to help and protect his dad from the dangers of the woods.

I HAVE THE GREATEST DAD
(Sung to "Mary Had a Little Lamb")

I know I have the greatest dad,
Greatest dad, greatest dad.
I know I have the greatest dad
In the whole wide world.

He loves to spend his time with me,
Time with me, time with me.
He loves to spend his time with me
When he comes home from work.

We joke and play and run around,
Run around, run around.
We joke and play and run around
As often as we can.

We talk and read and hug so tight,
Hug so tight, hug so tight.
We talk and read and hug so tight
Before I go to bed.

He makes me smile and feel so good,
Feel so good, feel so good.
He makes me smile and feel so good,
And I love him so!

RECIPES

SUNRISE SANDWICHES

Prepare this breakfast treat for your child to share with her dad on his special day.

1. Preheat oven to 325 degrees.
2. Cut a 1-inch-deep hole in the center of 2 whole unsliced hamburger buns, but don't go through the bottom.
3. Lift out the circle with a fork; butter the inside of the opening.
4. Place the buns on a cookie sheet; drop an egg into each hole.
5. Bake for 25 minutes.
6. Top the egg bun with a slice of American cheese.
7. Bake 5 minutes more. Serve immediately.

DADDY SNACK

Make this yummy mixture, then bag it into small portions. Tie each one up with a ribbon to make it airtight, then enclose it with Dad's invitation gift (see Activities below).

1. Spread 4 cups of bite-size shredded wheat on a cookie sheet. Cover with 1/3 cup melted margarine. Bake at 350 degrees for 15 minutes.
2. Add 1 1/2 cup sesame sticks, 1/2 cup raw peanuts, and 1/2 cup dried fruit.
3. Mix well.

ACTIVITIES

FATHER'S DAY CARD

Fold a piece of colored construction paper in half. On the outside glue a picture of Dad alone or Dad with his children. If you don't have a picture that you can use, have your child draw his own impression of his dad. Let him decorate the edges as he wishes, and on the inside of the card print, "Anyone can be a father. But it takes someone special to be a daddy!" Have your child sign it and add any other decorations he'd like.

DADDY INVITATIONS

1. Choose paper and markers that will look as polished and ornate as possible—perhaps some black construction paper with gold or silver ink, or some nice stationery with a calligraphy pen—whatever your child likes.

2. Fold the paper in half.

3. On the outside portion, write the following:

You are invited . . . .

4. On the inside section, write one of the following:
- ■ on one evening walk with me.
- ■ to go camping in the back yard with me.
- ■ to go on one bike hike with me.
- ■ to go to the park for a picnic with me.

—or any other activity that your child would love to do with just her dad.

5. Have your child add stickers, illustrations, or other decorations as she sees fit.

6. Put the invitation (or invitations, if she wants to do more than one) in a box along with the Daddy Snack from the above recipe to be enjoyed as an energy boost during the outing.

7. Wrap up the gift with the Daddy Wrapping Paper as suggested below.

DADDY WRAPPING PAPER

1. Have your child think of a simple symbol that represents her dad (i.e., tennis racquet, racquetball racquet, golf ball, car, tie, glasses, basketball, the letters "Dad").

2. Cut a potato in half. Draw the symbol on the cut potato half, and then carve the symbol out.

3. Have your child dip the potato carving into ink or paint and press it onto butcher paper or even a cut-open grocery bag.

4. Once it has dried, use it as Dad's personalized wrapping paper.

THIRD WEEK

Have a Summer Pancake Celebration

School is out. The morning rush is temporarily over. For several glorious months the first sound of the morning doesn't have to be your alarm clock, beckoning you at an untimely hour to get your family up and going. (Perhaps you can stay in bed until they are up and going all on their own!) Morning can be a peaceful and relaxing time of day once again.

Breakfast takes on a new meaning now, too. Eating on the run can be replaced by leisurely sitting down together to enjoy a plate of perfect pancakes. The beauty of pancakes is that they are appetizing at any time of the morning. So, please, indulge in a late morning sleep, and then when everyone is hungry and ready, celebrate the beginning of your summer vacation together with a pleasant pancake breakfast.

READINGS

Pancakes for Breakfast by Tomie de Paola (Harcourt, Brace, Jovanovich)

This wordless picture book needs no words to convey its humor. When a little old lady tries to

make some pancakes for her breakfast, she encounters several obstacles. But she overcomes them and in the process demonstrates a very important lesson: "If at first you don't succeed, try try again."

Pancakes Pancakes by Eric Carle (Alfred A. Knopf)

When Jack wakes up one morning he is hungry for a large pancake. But before he can have one he must help his mom get all the ingredients—by cutting the wheat, grinding it to flour, feeding the hens to get an egg, and milking the cow. The reader will grow to appreciate the advantages of our modern-day supermarkets by the end of this story.

The Pancake King by Phyllis LaFarge (Delacorte Press)

It all begins one morning when Henry Edgewood makes himself some pancakes for breakfast. He likes them so much that he continues making them for every meal, every day, for everyone. He gets really good at it, and eventually a talent scout scoops him up and makes him rich and famous. But Henry loses interest when he begins to miss his family, friends, and school, and his pancakes take second place.

RECITINGS

A PANCAKE SONG
(Sung to "Sing a Song of Sixpence")

Sing a song of pancakes,
A special breakfast treat—
Blueberry, banana,
So tasty and so sweet.
I can't make up my mind
Which one I like the best;
I guess I'll have to try each one,
To give them a taste test!

HAVE YOU EVER HAD A PANCAKE?
(Sung to "Did You Ever See a Lassie?")

Have you ever had a pancake,
A pancake, a pancake—
Have you ever had a pancake
That tasted so good?
I mixed it and stirred it
And popped it in the pan,
Then I cooked it to perfection.
Oh, isn't it grand!

RECIPES

HOMEMADE PANCAKES
1. Sift together 1 cup flour, 1 1/2 teaspoons baking powder, 1 tablespoon sugar, and 1/2 teaspoon salt.
2. Beat 2 eggs lightly.
3. Pour eggs, 1/2 cup milk, and 2 tablespoons melted margarine into flour mixture.
4. Mix only long enough to blend. Batter should be lumpy.
5. Cook on a hot griddle.

6. Now here comes the fun. Right after you've poured the batter onto the hot griddle, your child can add any or all of the following to design his very own original pancake. He can choose from

■ sliced fresh strawberries—super this time of year;

■ sliced or mashed bananas, blueberries, peaches, apples, or any other fresh fruit he'd like;

■ raisins, chopped nuts, coconut, cinnamon;

or anything else you might think of.

Let him arrange the ingredients in rows, letter shapes, dots, or other similar ideas, being creative and just having fun.

There are even different ways to serve the pancakes. Roll them up and stuff them with fruit salad, applesauce, or cottage cheese. Layer them and spread cream cheese or peanut butter on each layer. Or top them with jams, honey, or syrups.

POTATOCHEZ PANCAKES
1. Blend 2 eggs and 2 teaspoons milk.
2. Stir in 2 large, grated potatoes, 1/2 cup grated mild cheddar cheese, and 2 tablespoons flour.
3. Drop by spoonfuls onto a greased frying pan or griddle. Fry until light brown on each side.
    Makes 10 small pancakes.

HAVE A PANCAKE PARTY

Everyone loves parties and everyone loves pancakes. So add some of the extra touches listed below and make your breakfast into an exciting family party.

Make Pancake Place Mats (see activities below) and decorate the table with them. Finish setting the table with silverware, cups, and napkins.

Now, for the cooking! Either have the batter prepared in advance or have each person contribute some ingredient to make it a joint effort. Have all of the creative ingredients prepared ahead of time in separate bowls so that each person can select what he wishes to use. If the children are too young, you will need to pour the batter onto the hot griddle and take orders for each creative pancake. Otherwise, allow each person to do his own creating.

Enjoy your pancakes together. You may wish to try bites of each other's pancake to sample many different combinations and decide on your favorites.

After the feasting is over and all is cleaned up, play the two games mentioned in the activities below.

PANCAKE PLACE MATS

Have enough poster board or heavy construction paper to cut out a large circle for each person. Have everyone decorate her own circle as the type of pancake she wishes to eat today (for example, draw on red strawberry slices, peach slices, and blueberry dots for a fruity pancake). Cover each place mat with clear contact paper to protect it from spills.

PANCAKE TOSS

Have 3 five-inch diameter circles cut out of poster board. Decorate them as pancakes. Cover with contact paper if you wish. (Do this ahead of time or have each child make one or two—you can have more than three, if you wish.)

Get a large bowl, basket, or pail.

Stand approximately 5 feet back from the basket. Put a marker on the floor to section this off.

Throw the "pancakes" like Frisbees to try to get them into the container.

Each person gets three tries (or more, depending on how many "pancakes" you made).

PANCAKE MATCHING CARD GAME

Make as many pancakes as you wish, being sure to make two of each design that you draw (for example, two blueberry ones, two strawberry ones, two chopped nuts ones).

Use them as a card game. Deal all the cards out. Play like Old Maid, where you try to make as many matches as possible. Whoever has the most number of matches when all the cards are gone, wins.

FOURTH WEEK

Pond Life Fun

Summertime is a wondrous time of year for water play. Aside from the obvious water sports available to us all, ponds spring to life and offer a myriad of exciting things to see and do. We can see all kinds of water creatures and study their birth, growth, and habits. One thrilling inhabitant to observe is the frog. Children find it electrifying to catch a tadpole in a bucket and watch it wiggle around in the water. Development from eggs to tadpoles to full-grown frogs takes just two to three months, so it's possible to observe a full life cycle with just a few visits to a nearby pond.

Obviously the most appropriate project in dealing with pond life is to visit a pond as often as you can, carefully observing what is there and what changes have taken place since your previous visit. Take buckets and nets to help your child scoop.

This chapter offers some things to do to follow up on your trips to the pond.

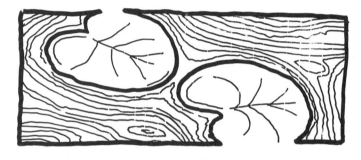

READINGS

The Mysterious Tadpole by Steven Kellogg (Dial)

Louis receives his birthday gift from his uncle in Scotland—a tadpole. This creature has lots of surprises in store for Louis because it deviates from the normal growth pattern of tadpoles. Steven Kellogg's humorous illustrations are outdone only by his very clever and surprise ending.

The Pond by Carol and Donald Carrick (The Macmillan Co.)

Dragonflies, fish, turtles, and frogs are some of the many inhabitants described in this book.

In the Pond by Ermanno Cristini (Picture Book Studio)

This wordless panoramic study of pond life has beautiful illustrations of the plants and animals that inhabit a pond.

RECITINGS

HOPPY
(Sung to "Bingo")

There was a boy who had a frog,
And Hoppy was his name, O!
H-O-P-P-Y, H-O-P-P-Y, H-O-P-P-Y,
And Hoppy was his name, O!

He found him in the pond one day,
A tiny little tadpole.
H-O-P-P-Y, H-O-P-P-Y, H-O-P-P-Y,
And Hoppy was his name, O!

He watched this tadpole every day,
And saw him grow in many ways.
H-O-P-P-Y, H-O-P-P-Y, H-O-P-P-Y,
And Hoppy was his name, O!

Then one great morn he saw it true,
His tadpole was a frog, brand new!
H-O-P-P-Y, H-O-P-P-Y, H-O-P-P-Y,
And Hoppy was his name, O!

FROGS
A frog begins his life in a pond
As he hatches out of his egg.
He learns to swim with his mighty tail
'Cause he has no arms or legs.
Several weeks pass, he eats and grows,
And his tail shrinks very small.
And then he grows some arms and legs,
So he can hop around and crawl.

RECIPES

Since a frog's diet mainly consists of bugs, "bug" recipes should be fun to make.

"BUGS" ON A LOG
Clean a stalk of celery, spread peanut butter in the groove, and place raisins on top of the peanut butter. That's it—Bugs (raisins) on a Log (celery with peanut butter)!

"BUG"-FILLED COOKIES
1. Preheat oven to 350 degrees.
2. Cream together ½ cup white or brown sugar and ½ cup margarine.
3. Beat in 2 eggs, 2½ cups flour, 2 teaspoons baking powder, and 1 teaspoon vanilla.
4. Chill dough 3 to 4 hours before rolling.
5. Roll dough thin and cut into rounds.
6. Place 1 tablespoon of the filling on top of one round, place a second round over the filling, and seal edges firmly by pressing them with a floured fork.
7. Bake for 20-25 minutes.
Makes about 20 2-inch filled cookies.

"BUG" (RAISIN) FILLING
Boil and stir until thick: 1 cup "bugs" (raisins), 6 tablespoons sugar, 5 tablespoons boiling water, ½ teaspoon grated lemon rind, 2 teaspoons lemon juice, 2 teaspoons margarine, and ⅛ teaspoon salt.

ACTIVITIES

MAKE A "HOPPY FROG"
1. Draw a simple frog on green construction paper (or white paper that can be colored in green).
2. To draw a frog: Begin with a large circle for the body. Add a small circle at a 2:00 and a 10:00 position for the two bug-out eyes. Add a leg with a webbed foot at the 4:00 and the 8:00 position. Add a half-circle at the 3:00 and the 9:00 position for the two hind legs. Add a big smile a little higher than halfway up in the circle.
3. Cut the frog out.
4. Make a spring to staple onto the back of the frog. Take an index card or other stiff paper and fold it accordion-style 8 to 10 times.
Now you have a homemade "hoppy" frog with which you can play all kinds of games.
Instead of attaching the springs to the bottom of the frog, you can also attach them to the top and use them as hangers for the frogs. Suspend them from the ceiling, lights, doorknobs, etc.

"HOPPY" FROG RACES
Encourage your child to play with her hoppy frogs. She can push down on the spring and see which one hops the farthest, blow them to see which one slides the farthest, snap them with her fingers to see which one glides the farthest, or any other ideas she may come up with.

LEAPFROG WITH THE HOPPY FROGS
See if your child can get her hoppy frogs to leap over each other in the same fashion that you would with another person.
Play leapfrog with your child and her friends and follow various trails and marked-out designs.

CHAPTER SEVEN

JULY

A Month to Celebrate Birthdays and the Great Outdoors

July appears on the calendar with fireworks and festivities, as Americans celebrate the birth of our country. While in the birthday frame of mind take a few extra moments to ponder your child's next birthday with some thoughts and suggestions offered in this chapter. Then it's off to some typical summertime outdoor favorites: spending a day at the beach, spending a night sleeping out under the stars, and observing nature's nighttime lighting—fireflies.
For each of these summer treats you will find plenty of activities.

FIRST WEEK

Happy Birthday, America

Those of us who have lived in the United States all of our lives take our country somewhat for granted. The freedoms that we've grown up with have become second nature to us. Things as simple as reading an unbiased newspaper, speaking freely about what we believe, attending the college of our choice, and having an abundance and selection of food and clothing are just a few of our many American liberties.

But there have been, and continue to be, people from all over the world who leave all they have ever known and owned to face the uncertainty of "making it" in America. They all hope and pray that they'll find a better life in this land of opportunity.

July 4 is the celebration of the birth of our country. On this day, Americans traditionally celebrate America's birthday with parades, fireworks, picnics, patriotic speeches, and the unfurling of the national American flag.

Fourth of July by Barbara M. Joosse (Knopf)

Ross is five years old and feels he isn't allowed to do much. His parents keep telling him to wait until he is six. But there is one thing he will be allowed to do this year: he can carry the banner in the Fourth of July parade. Little does he realize just how difficult a job this is. But his determination to prove his abilities keeps him going and helps him to succeed.

Henry's Fourth of July by Holly Keller (Greenwillow Books)

Everything about Henry's Fourth of July celebration is perfect—the parade, the potato sack races, the picnic, and especially the fireworks. The only sad thing about the day is that it is over too quickly.

READINGS

RECITINGS

Watch the Stars Come Out by Riki Levinson (E.P. Dutton)

In this book a little red-headed girl tells of her trip to join her mama and papa, who have already immigrated to America. Lonely and fearful, she boards a boat with strangers for the three-week voyage, but she is rewarded in the end by the thrills of seeing America for the first time and being reunited with her parents.

JULY FOURTH
(Sung to "Pop! Goes The Weasel")
All around the United States
Americans will celebrate—
With picnics, flags, and fancy parades,
And the pop! of the fireworks!

AMERICA THE BEAUTIFUL

O beautiful for spacious skies,
For amber waves of grain,
For purple mountain majesties
Above the fruited plain.
America! America!
God shed His grace on thee,
And crown thy good
With brotherhood
From sea to shining sea.

This song was written in 1893 by Katherine Lee Bates, an English professor at Wellesley College. Shortly before writing it she had been on a trip out West and had seen "spacious skies" and "fruited plains" while looking from the summit of Pike's Peak.

If your child finds some of these lyrics too difficult to understand, please take a few minutes to explain them. They truly are magnificent; once they are explained, your child, too, will love this song about our grand country.

RECIPES

AMERICAN PATRIOTIC BERRIES

This easy, red-white-and-blue snack is a tasty patriotic treat.

1. Wash 3 strawberries and 8 blueberries. Put them in a cup.
2. Sprinkle with shredded coconut.
3. Add a dollop of vanilla, strawberry, or blueberry yogurt.

STATUE OF LIBERTY CAKE

Another simple dessert, impressive and festive.

1. Bake your favorite cake—either a box cake or one of your own recipes.
2. Pour the batter into one 8-inch round cake pan and one 8-inch square cake pan.
3. Bake the desired amount of time and allow to cool.
4. Use the round cake as the head of the Statue of Liberty and place it on a large serving tray.
5. Cut the square cake into 7 triangles to use as the points of the crown. (To get 7 triangles, cut a W and a V next to each other.)
6. Arrange the triangles around the circle.
7. Frost and decorate as desired.

ACTIVITIES

PATRIOTIC STRAW PAINTING

Do this activity outdoors; you may wish to have your child wear some type of smock.

1. Pour 3 small, separate circles of poster paints in the center of a large piece of paper (12 by 18 inches). Use one circle of each of the following colors: red, white and blue.
2. Give your child a straw and have him spread the paint around by blowing through the straw or by using the tip of the straw as a paintbrush.

This activity might be messy, but what fun!

FOURTH OF JULY FIRECRACKERS

Outdoors might be best for this activity, too!

1. Roll up red construction paper to make a tube 6 inches long and 3 inches in diameter. Fasten with tape.

2. Have your child decorate it with gold stars, American flag stickers, or other festive decorations.

3. Cut 2 circles the same circumference of the tube and put a hole in the center of one. Insert a few inches of string and tape firmly on one side for the firecracker "wick."

4. Use tape to hook this circle hinge-fashion to one open end of the tube.

5. Securely tape the other circle to the other end.

6. Let your child fill the tube with homemade confetti, made by punching out red, white, and blue circles with a paper punch.

Enjoy.

AMERICAN FLAGS

Together with your child, make one or the other or both of these simple American flags.

1. Tape red, white, and blue streamers to a stick or ruler. Hold it up high and wave it in the breeze.

2. Cut a rectangular piece of white poster board. Measure off a box at the top left-hand side for the stars, and thirteen stripes. Have your child color in seven red stripes, leaving every other stripe white. Draw in 50 blue stars, or color that section blue and glue on 50 gold sticker stars.

SECOND WEEK

Celebrating Your Child's Day of All Days

The day one is born is certainly great cause for celebrating. All of us want to be able to give our children the most memorable, fun-filled day ever on their birthdays. It is truly their day and even though we want them to always feel special, on their birthdays they should feel like princes or princesses. This chapter will give you some birthday suggestions that you might be able to stow away until your child's next birthday.

READINGS	RECITINGS

Happy Birthday to You by Dr. Seuss (Random House)

This fantastic book celebrates a child's birthday by portraying everything a child might ever dream of doing or having on her birthday. It is fascinating to read—perhaps a bit too long for some young listeners, but Dr. Seuss's incredible characters and imagination will delight all who love birthdays. (And who doesn't?!)

The Secret Birthday Message by Eric Carle (Thomas Y. Crowell Co.; pb Harper Junior Books)

This book is rather brief, but the story and idea presented here make it another favorite.

The book begins with a secret message for Tim on the eve of his birthday. The message takes him on a treasure hunt to find his birthday present. The children will thrill at deciphering the message, following Tim on his hunt, and sharing in the excitement of finding the birthday surprise.

Happy Birthday, Moon by Frank Asch (Prentice-Hall)

Bear and the moon seem to have something in common—their birthdays! Bear learns all he wishes to know about the moon's birthday wishes when he holds a priceless "echo" conversation with the moon.

BIRTHDAY CHILD
(Sung to "London Bridge")

Aren't you glad that you were born,
You were born, you were born—
Aren't you glad that you were born,
Birthday child?

Every year we celebrate,
Celebrate, celebrate—
Every year we celebrate,
Birthday child.

Birthday parties are such fun,
Are such fun, are such fun—
Birthday parties are such fun,
Birthday child.

Balloons and games for everyone,
Everyone, everyone—
Balloons and games for everyone,
Birthday child.

Cake and ice cream are such treats,
Are such treats, are such treats—
Cake and ice cream are such treats,
Birthday child.

But more than any of these things,
Of these things, of these things—
More than any of these things,
Birthday child . . .

We're so glad that you were born,
You were born, you were born—
We're so glad that you were born,
Because we love you!

THIS YOUNG BOY
(Sung to "This Old Man")

This young boy, when he turned one,
We couldn't believe one year had gone,
With a knick-knack-patty-whack, we're so proud
    of you,
Happy birthday, we love you!

This young boy, when he turned two,
He'd grown so tall and handsome, too,
With a knick-knack-patty-whack, we're so proud
    of you,
Happy birthday, we love you!

This young boy, when he turned three,
He shared his cake with his guests and me,
With a knick-knack-patty-whack, we're so proud
    of you,
Happy birthday, we love you!

This young boy, when he turned four,
We hid his presents behind the door,
With a knick-knack-patty-whack, we're so proud
    of you,
Happy birthday, we love you!

This young boy, now you're five,
Isn't it great to be alive?!
With a knick-knack-patty-whack, we're so proud
    of you,
Happy birthday, we love you!

(Change the words to this song to fit your child's situation. Obviously, if your child is a girl, the lyrics will be, "This young girl, she turned . . ." Also, if your child is celebrating her fourth birthday, make that the last verse and change it to, "This young girl, now you're four, / What can you find behind the door?" after you've hidden something there for her!)

RECIPES

BIRTHDAY BANANA CAKE

1. Preheat oven to 350 degrees.
2. Sift 2¼ cups flour, ½ teaspoon baking powder, ¾ teaspoon baking soda, and ¼ teaspoon salt.
3. Mash 1 cup ripe bananas (2-3 bananas) and add 1 teaspoon vanilla and ¼ cup vanilla yogurt to the bananas.
4. Cream until very light ½ cup margarine and ½ cup sugar. Add 2 eggs. Beat in well.
5. Add ⅓ of the flour mixture to the margarine mixture. Stir well. Next add ½ of the banana mixture. Repeat with the flour mixture and the banana mixture and end with the flour mixture. Stir until smooth.
6. Bake in two 9-inch round greased pans for about 30 minutes.
7. When cool, frost with a frosting of your choice and decorate as you wish.

BIRTHDAY SANDWICHES

Children are proud of how old they are on their birthdays, so make their sandwiches in the shape of their new age. Try making a French Toast-Grilled Cheese Sandwich as a special treat. First make 2 pieces of French toast; put 2 slices of cheese (and ham, optional) inside; butter lightly on the outside; then grill it. Remember to cut it into a 5 or 6 or whatever age your child has just turned.

ACTIVITIES

BIRTHDAY HUNT

Treasure hunts are fun for children; plan to have an extra special birthday hunt. There are various ways to do a hunt; select one that is most appropriate for you.

1. Follow the pattern of *The Secret Birthday Message* and write a coded letter for your child to decipher. The letter might read something like this: "When you get out of bed, take three giant steps toward the hallway. Take a right turn and walk until you can go no farther. Open the door in front of you. Hop down five steps. Turn left. Take ten steps until you reach a tree. Look up. Climb up three branches and look down across the yard until you see something wrapped up for you. Carefully get down and go open up your gift!"

2. Write up a series of notes and hide them in various locations around the house and yard. For example, the first one might say, "Go to the refrigerator" (you can use picture clues and draw simple sketches of the various places he is to go). When he gets to the refrigerator, he will find another clue taped there. That one might say, "Go to the bathtub," and so on.

Find whichever method is comfortable for you and have fun setting the hunt up. You may wish to do it immediately once your child gets up, or save it for another time of the day.

MY BIRTHDAY BOOK

This project may very well turn out to be an annual birthday treat.

1. Gather pictures of your child doing special things that he enjoyed during the past year. Choose approximately 10.
2. Cut poster board or other sturdy paper to a size and shape you'd like.
3. Lay out the pictures in an order that you like, think of captions for each, and then begin assembling your book.
4. Glue the pictures, write the captions, then cover each page with clear contact paper.
5. Tape all the pages together with colorful cloth tape, adhering two pages together at a time. You may also wish to use the tape around the other 3 sides of each page to give the book a more finished and polished look.
6. Call it simply "Morgan's Book—Volume 1" and do an update each year. It's a great way to see yearly activities and changes and your child will treasure this book more than any other because he is the star! You can either do this together or as a surprise for his birthday.

MY ARTWORK SCRAPBOOK

This is a great way to save your child's favorite artwork from year to year.

1. During the year have a special place to put all the artwork that comes home from school, library story-hour, church school, or other such place. (A drawer or a box would be fine.)
2. Before birthday time, weed through this drawer with your child and decide together which pictures are the most special. Save these and compile them into a scrapbook. You may have to help quite a bit in determining a certain number of pictures to keep, as your child may wish to save every single one.
3. Either purchase an inexpensive scrapbook or make one out of a notebook or binder.

THIRD WEEK

Let's Spend a Day at the Beach

Why is going to the beach such a treasured summer outing? Perhaps it is because there is something for everyone at the beach. For some people it is the smell and gentle caress of the ocean breeze; for others it's the intense warmth of the glowing sun. For some people the beach connotes total relaxation in the sun; for others it means adventure on the water. For some people it's a day to be a child again and build the sand castle of their dreams; and for others it's a day to frolic in the waves. Whatever going to the beach does for you, plan a beach day and have fun together.

READINGS

Harry by the Sea by Gene Zion (Harper Junior Books)

When Harry, a black and white dog, joins his family on a beach outing, he finds the sun a bit too hot. His deliberate attempts to get cool are overshadowed when an ocean wave crashes over him and he emerges as a seaweed-covered seamonster. Now Harry is no longer hot, but he has two bigger problems: he must escape being captured as a rare sea creature and he must find his family from whom he has strayed. This, the fourth story that Harry has starred in, is just as funny and enjoyable as the other three crazy adventures.

When the Tide Is Low by Sheila Cole (Lothrop, Lee & Shepard Books)

A little girl and her mom talk about all the things they will see when they go out to play on the beach. But they must wait for when the tide is low—and that seems like an eternity to an anxious little girl.

A Day at the Beach by Mircea Vasiliu (Random House)

A family of five who spends an entire day at the beach enjoys everything from frolicking in the water and building sand castles to collecting shells and treasures and going clamming.

RECITINGS

WE'RE GOING TO THE BEACH
(Sung to "Farmer in the Dell")
We're going to the beach,
We're going to the beach,
Hi-ho the derry-o,
We're going to the beach.
We'll pack a picnic lunch, *(etc.)*
We'll wear our bathing suits, *(etc.)*
We'll bring our water toys, *(etc.)*
We'll splash around and swim, *(etc.)*

We'll find some rocks and shells, *(etc.)*

We'll build a great sand castle, *(etc.)*

We'll fly the highest kite, *(etc.)*

We'll get so tan all over, *(etc.)*

We'll have a super day! *(etc.)*

WE ALL LOVE THE BEACH

We all love the beach;
It's a great place to go.
But what are the reasons
That make this so?

"Collecting sand dollars," Matthew says with a smile.
Jogging is mom's favorite, for one or two miles.
Splashing in the waves is Michael's first choice;
Shouting to the seagulls in Kyle's loudest voice.

Flying a kite makes Dad's spirits soar,
And hearing the ocean surf pound and roar,
Feeling the warmth and glow from the sun,
Feeling content when day is all done.

RECIPES

Make these two cookie recipes and bring them along to the beach.

BASEBALL COOKIES

1. Mix together ½ cup wheat germ, 1½ cups peanut butter, 1½ cups honey, 3 cups dried milk, and ¾ cup graham cracker crumbs.
2. Form into balls like large marbles. Roll in confectioner's sugar or shredded coconut.
3. Refrigerate.

BEACHY CHEWS

1. Preheat oven to 350 degrees.
2. Cream ½ cup margarine and ¾ cup sugar.

3. Add 2 well-beaten eggs, then 1 cup flour, ½ teaspoon salt, and 1 teaspoon vanilla.
4. Fold in 1 cup finely-cut dates (or apricots) and 1 cup chopped walnuts.
5. Bake in a well-buttered 9-by-9-inch pan for 25-30 minutes.
6. Cool. Cut in squares or strips.

ACTIVITIES

BEACH TREASURE HUNT

There are many treasures to find on a beach. Give your child a pail and have her casually look for whatever happens to come her way. Or, be more specific and give her an actual list of things to try to locate, such as a piece of driftwood, seaweed, a sand dollar, a starfish, and various sizes, shapes, and colors of shells.

BEACH RUBBINGS

Take some of the beach treasures your child found and do the following project: Put the treasure on the table, cover it with a piece of thin, white paper, then rub over it with crayons. Use a new piece of paper for each object, label it on the back, then play a guessing game trying to figure out what each rubbing belongs to.

SHELL PROJECTS

Have your child gather as many shells as he can find at the beach. Then have fun with the following activities:

■ Set out pairs of different kinds of shells in random order. Have your child match the shells that are alike.

■ Have your child glue small shells or shell pieces to heavy paper, cardboard, or paper plates to make shell collages.

■ Place all the shells in a bucket and have your child guess how many shells he thinks are in the bucket. After the guessing, count them to see how close he came.

■ Hide an object under one of three shells lined up in a row. Then move the shells around and have your child guess which shell the object is hidden under.

FOURTH WEEK

Camping-Out Fun for the Whole Family

Do you remember the very first time you camped out under the stars? Did you spend the night with your brother or sister, your mom or dad, or a friend, or alone? Were you in your own back yard or somewhere farther away? What did you take with you? Did you have a midnight snack? Do you remember the color of your sleeping bag or how soft the inside of it felt? Were you ever scared? Did you make it through the whole night? How did you feel in the morning—tired . . . stiff . . . proud?

Maybe your camp reminiscing will uncover happy memories of times you enjoyed sleeping out as a child. This chapter's activities will help you plan a successful campout experience for your child so that someday she will be able to smile when she reminisces about the first time she camped out under the stars.

READINGS

Pip Camps Out by Myra Berry Brown (Golden Gate Junior Books)

"Why can't I go to camp and sleep in a sleeping bag?" Pip asks his mom as he watches his big sister ride off to camp. Pip is too young to go to an overnight camp but he is just the right age to have his first sleep-out in his own back yard. This gentle story tells all about Pip's preparations and feelings as he experiences his very first night under the stars.

Sleep Out by Donald and Carol Carrick (Seabury Press)

When Christopher gets a sleeping bag for his birthday he can't wait to try it out. His first solo camp-out experience is a real adventure—one that helps him decide to include Dad on the next sleep-out.

The Night We Slept Outside by Anne and Harlow Rockwell (Macmillan)

The first night that Robert and his brother get to sleep outside on their deck they hear sounds and see things they never knew existed in their night-time backyard.

RECITINGS

CAMPING, CAMPING
(Sung to "Yankee Doodle")

Camping, camping, I can't wait
To go sleep out tonight,
It's so neat
To fall asleep
Under the pale moonlight.

Camping, camping, it is great,
I'll take some snacks along,
Flashlight, compass, harmonica,
To play this little song.

THERE WAS ONE SLEEPING OUT
(Sung to "Roll Over")

There was one sleeping out,
But he soon called out
For others, for others,
So one answered his shout.
Now this song is about . . .

There were two sleeping out,
But they soon called out
For others, for others,
So one answered their shouts.
Now this song is about . . .

There were three sleeping out,
But they soon called out
For others, for others,
So one answered their shouts.
Now this song is about . . .

Continue up to ten and end with:
There were ten sleeping out,
And they soon called out,
"ZZZZZZZZZZ!"

RECIPES

Prepare these snacks for your child's big night out. They are tasty and nutritious and can second as breakfast treats as well.

CHEWY CHEWIES
1. Mix together 1/2 cup peanut butter and 2 tablespoons honey in a saucepan.
2. Beat in 2 eggs, one at a time. Stir constantly over medium heat, until the mixture boils and leaves the sides of the pan.
3. Remove from heat and stir in 2 tablespoons margarine and 2 teaspoons vanilla.
4. Add 1 1/2 cups raw oatmeal and 1 1/2 cups nuts (any selection or combination of nuts and/or dried fruit you'd prefer—for example, sunflower seeds, walnuts, cashews, almonds, raisins).
5. Mix together well and press mixture into an 8-inch square pan. Chill. Cut into bars.

SPECIAL CHIP MUFFINS
1. Preheat oven to 400 degrees.
2. Beat 3 tablespoons vegetable oil, 1 egg, 1 cup water, 1/4 cup honey, and 1/2 teaspoon vanilla.
3. Combine 1 cup minus 2 tablespoons whole wheat flour, 1 cup minus 2 tablespoons white flour, 1/4 teaspoon salt, 3 teaspoons baking powder, 3/4 cups rolled oats, 1/4 cup dry milk powder, and 1 teaspoon cinnamon. Add this to the wet ingredients. Stir to moisten only.
4. Fold in 1/2 cup chopped walnuts and 1/2 cup carob or chocolate chips.
5. Bake in greased muffin tins for 15-20 minutes. Makes 12 muffins.

PLANS FOR A REAL CAMPOUT

These plans can be used whether your child plans to "camp out" on the living room floor, on the screened-in porch, or in your back yard.

Gather the following supplies: sleeping bag (or a pillow and several blankets), flashlight, harmonica, snacks (see recipes above, and perhaps add some fresh fruit, too), and a canteen filled with water or a favorite juice.

Brush up on some campfire songs that you will be able to teach to or share with your child. One good source if your memory is a little cloudy is **Wee Sing Around the Campfire**, *by Pamela Conn Beall. Several titles that may jar your memory are "Clementine," "Down by the Old Mill Stream," "I've Been Working on the Railroad," "Jacob's Ladder," "Bingo," and of course, "Taps":*

Day is done, gone the sun,
From the lake, from the hill, from the sky.
All is well, safely rest, God is nigh.

You may wish to accompany some of these on a harmonica as your child sings along—or he may do the playing.

ACTIVITIES

FLASHLIGHT GAMES

Shadow Pictures

Show your child how to make shadow pictures. With your hands between the flashlight's light and a wall or tree, try casting shadows that look like animals. For example, to make a bunny, touch your thumb to your pinkie and ring fingers, and hold your index and middle fingers up.

Shadow Puppets

Trace animal-shaped cookie cutters onto stiff paper, cut them out, and punch holes for eyes with a paper punch. Tape the animal shapes to popsicle sticks or straws. Your child can shine the flashlight on the puppets so that they will cast shadows on a wall or tree.

Flashlight Tag

One person is "it" and tries to "catch" the other players with the beam from his flashlight.

SCAVENGER HUNT

Scavenger hunts are fun to do whether you are camping indoors or outdoors. Make ahead of time a list of the items each camper will need to find. Some examples for indoor items could be a small toy, a sponge, a button, a washcloth, and a pencil. Outdoor items might include a twig with three branches, an acorn, a piece of litter, a sand toy, or a black pebble. For non-readers, make the list by drawing pictures of the items to be found. Give a copy of the list to each camper. The first one to find and bring all of the items to you is the winner.

KNOT TYING

Bring along several pieces of rope to practice knot tying. If you need brushing up on some of the knots, borrow a book from your library. Try to learn and demonstrate some of the following: the clove hitch, the square knot, the bowline, and the fisherman's knot.

FIFTH WEEK

Fireflies—A Summer Treat

Out of all the creepy-crawly, pesky, attacking bugs that invade our privacy in the summer, there is one insect that people genuinely love—the firefly. Fireflies don't crawl up our legs, fly in our ears and eyes, or bite us to make us itch. Instead they put on a spectacular light show every summer evening for free. Who hasn't marveled at their unending source of energy? Who hasn't danced in the dark with them, jar in hand, trying to catch some (but promising to let them free after a few moments of a private glow show)?

READINGS

Fireflies! by Julie Brinckloe (Macmillan)

When a boy spots fireflies flickering outdoors one summer night, he dashes out to join his friends. Each, with a jar in hand, catches as many fireflies as he can before being called inside for bed. "I caught hundreds!" the boy reports to his family. But his excitement wanes as he notices a problem with the captured fireflies and must make a difficult decision.

Sam and the Firefly by P.D. Eastman (Beginner)

When Sam, an owl, meets Gus, a firefly, they spend night after night playing with Gus's spectacular light. Sam leads the way, Gus follows, and they make shapes, pictures, and words in the nighttime sky. The fun continues until Gus decides to play several unkind tricks with his new-found powers and Sam has to try to stop him.

A Firefly Named Torchy by Bernard Waber (Houghton Mifflin Co.)

Torchy, the firefly, has a problem. He can't twinkle. His light is so strong and bright that he floods the field with light and upsets all the sleeping animals. How Torchy solves his problem and learns to accept himself for what he is makes this an insightful story.

RECITINGS

BLINK, BLINK, FIREFLY
(Sung to "Baa, Baa, Black Sheep")

Blink, blink, firefly,
Have you light for me?
Yes sir, yes sir,
Enough to help you see.

I'll blink on for you,
We can play some hide and seek,
But promise not to catch me
In a jar—I'll get too weak.

Blink, blink, firefly,
Let's have some fun tonight,
I promise not to catch you,
And things will be all right.

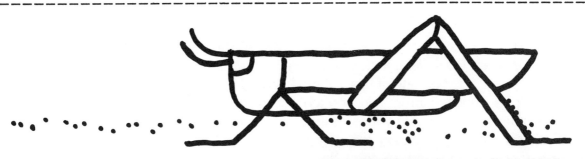

HUSH, LITTLE FIREFLY
(Sung to "Hush, Little Baby")

Hush, little firefly, don't you cry,
I'm not going to catch you, no not I;
I know you love to fly so free,
And I just want to watch, you see.

The way you light up amazes me,
You have such strength but you're so tiny;
How do you do it, I wish I knew,
Then I could fly around the skies with you.

RECIPES

"FIREFLY" JELL-O

Have your child use his imagination and pretend the Jell-O is the nighttime sky and the pineapple tidbits are the fireflies.

1. Sprinkle 2 packages of unflavored gelatin over 1 cup of grape juice in a small saucepan. Stir constantly over low heat until gelatin dissolves.
2. Remove pan from heat and add 3 cups more of grape juice.
3. Add 1 large can of unsweetened pineapple tidbits and stir in. Lemon peel may also be used.
4. Pour into a mold or bowl. Refrigerate to set.
   Makes 8 servings.

"FIREFLY" PEANUT CLUSTERS

1. Mix 1 cup sugar, 1/4 cup margarine, and 1/3 cup evaporated milk in a saucepan. Bring to a rolling boil and boil for 3 minutes, stirring frequently.
2. Remove from heat and stir in 1/4 cup crunchy peanut butter and 1/2 teaspoon vanilla.
3. Fold in 1 cup uncooked rolled oats and 1/2 cup Spanish peanuts.
4. Drop by tablespoons onto waxed paper on a baking sheet.
5. Let stand until set. Refrigerate.

ACTIVITIES

"BUG HOUSES"

Here are several ways to make little "bug houses" for your child to use to examine his insect findings, whether they are fireflies or other insects.

1. The simplest—take a wide-mouth jar of any size, punch a few holes in the lid for air.
2. Cut a square hole in the side of a quart or half-gallon milk carton. Tape a piece of nylon net or plastic screening over the hole to make a window for viewing your insects. Put the insects in from the top. Use a paper clip to secure the top edges and to keep the bugs inside until it's time to free them.
3. Long boxes such as the ones spaghetti and lasagna come in, with cellophane windows, can serve as temporary shelters for grasshoppers or caterpillars.

ANT HOMES

If your child wishes to watch ants, here's a great home to make for them. Put several inches of dirt or sand in a one-gallon jar. Make sure it has a good lid with a few holes punched in it. Add enough water to dampen the soil, then put in your ants and some food. Be careful not to put in too much food—just a few crumbs or a tiny piece of hamburger. Add a piece of absorbent cotton and keep it damp by adding a few drops of water to it each day. This home will suffice for several days or weeks, and it will be fun to watch the ants live and work in it.

WATERLENS

To observe water bugs, make this handy piece of equipment.

Take a large plastic pail and cut the bottom out of it. Stretch a piece of plastic wrap loosely over the top of the pail and fasten it with a rubber band. Have your child place the end with the plastic wrap into the water. As she looks through the cut-off bottom-end, she should be able to see what's going on under the water.

WATERSCOPE

Using the same materials you can also make a waterscope that will be fun to observe things through.

Take a large plastic pail and cut two or three holes in the sides of the pail. Then stretch some plastic wrap loosely over the top of the pail and fasten it with a rubber band. Fill the top cavity with water. Have your child hold objects that she wishes to examine inside the holes you made, under the plastic wrap, and study them.

CHAPTER EIGHT

AUGUST

A Month of Cures for the Late Summer Doldrums

All the enthusiasm and pent-up energy that children pour into the month of June has a tendency to dwindle down to a trickle in August. This is the month one might hear tones of boredom and see signs of restlessness.

The ideas offered in this chapter should give you plenty of things to help your child continue to reap the benefits of the precious summer season. Whether you get into berry picking, joke telling, item collecting, or tall tale telling, delight in the remainder of the summer with your child.

FIRST WEEK

Blueberries for All

Blueberry season is upon us, and for blueberry lovers the next few weeks will be filled with breakfasts of blueberry-speckled cereal and blueberry muffins; lunches of blueberry bread spread with blueberry jam; dinners of chicken blueberry; and bedtime snacks of blueberries in cream. (Perhaps it's a good thing that the blueberry season is so short!) Whether you purchase your blueberries at the grocery store or pick your own at a nearby farm, do get some before the season is over. There are several activities below that will bring out the blueberry in you as you have fun doing them with your child.

READINGS

Blueberries for Sal by Robert McCloskey (Viking; pb Penguin)

Little Sal and her mother go to Blueberry Hill one day to gather blueberries for the winter. Little Bear and his mother also go to Blueberry Hill to store up food for the winter. When Little Sal and Little Bear wander off from their mothers' sides only to turn up with the opposite mother, the blueberry picking is comically halted.

The Blueberry Cake That Little Fox Baked by Andrea Da Rif (Margaret K. McElderry Books)

Little Fox bakes a blueberry cake, thinking that it is his mother's birthday, when actually it is Blueberry Day. The trouble he innocently gets himself into is smoothed out and all ends well.

The Blueberry Bears by Eleanor Lapp (Albert Whitman)

In this story Bessie Allen learns not to stockpile blueberries. The logical conclusion will bring a smile to all.

RECITINGS

BLUEBERRY PICKING

Have you ever gone blueberry picking
On a warm sweet August day?
You say you've not? Two pails I've got—
Take one and join me today!

Just wait till you see the blueberries,
So plump and purplish blue.
I bet you'll want to eat every one
You pick—it's hard not to!

Just wait till you taste the blueberries,
Fresh and juicy and sweet,
Then and only then you'll know
Why picking them is such a treat.

HERE WE GO 'ROUND THE BLUEBERRY BUSH
(Sung to "Here We Go 'Round the Mulberry Bush")

Here we go 'round the blueberry bush,
The blueberry bush, the blueberry bush.
Here we go 'round the blueberry bush,
Picking yummy berries.

Berries to make some blueberry pies,
Blueberry pies, blueberry pies—
Blueberries to make some blueberry pies,
To share for you and me.

Berries to make some blueberry cakes,
Blueberry cakes, blueberry cakes—
Berries to make some blueberry cakes,
Such fun to mix and bake.

Berries to make some blueberry jam,
Blueberry jam, blueberry jam—
Berries to make some blueberry jam,
And see how proud I am!

Add other verses for other blueberry treats you make.

RECIPES

BLUEBERRY JAM

Undoubtedly you'll have no trouble finding recipes in which to use your blueberries. There are recipes for blueberry muffins, tarts, pies, cream pies, cakes, buckles, breads . . . and the list goes on. This recipe for Blueberry Jam was chosen because it is simple and quick yet exciting for kids to make and yummy to eat in a peanut butter sandwich or on pancakes.

1. Wash and mash $1\frac{1}{2}$ quarts of blueberries.
2. Measure $4\frac{1}{2}$ cups of the mashed blueberries into a large saucepan.
3. Squeeze the juice from 1 medium lemon and measure 2 tablespoons into the saucepan with the blueberries.
4. Add 7 cups of sugar. Stir to mix well. Then boil hard for 1 minute, stirring constantly.
5. Remove from heat and stir in 1 bottle of Certo.
6. Skim off foam with a metal spoon. Continue stirring and skimming for about 5 minutes to prevent the fruit from settling at the top.
7. Ladle into sterilized jars and cover immediately with $\frac{1}{8}$-inch hot paraffin.

BLUEBERRY-LEMON MUFFINS

This recipe was chosen because it is so-o-o good!

1. Preheat oven to 400 degrees.
2. Sift $1\frac{3}{4}$ cup flour, $\frac{1}{4}$ cup sugar, 2 teaspoons baking powder, and $\frac{1}{2}$ teaspoon salt into a mixing bowl. Make a well in the center.
3. Combine $\frac{3}{4}$ cup milk, 1 well-beaten egg, and $\frac{1}{3}$ cup oil. All at once add to the dry ingredients. Stir quickly, just till dry ingredients are moistened.
4. Toss together 1 cup blueberries, 1 teaspoon sugar, and 2 teaspoon grated lemon peel. Gently stir into batter.
5. Fill greased muffin tins $\frac{2}{3}$ full.
6. Bake for 25 minutes.

Makes 12 regular-sized muffins or 24 miniature ones.

ACTIVITIES

BLUEBERRY PICKING

If at all possible, go blueberry picking together. Even if you only last for half an hour and pick only half a pound of berries it'll be worth the time.

If you are unable to go blueberry picking, plan a pretend picking, using peanuts or other appropriate food. Simply hide the peanuts as you would for an Easter egg hunt, give each person a pail for his "pickings," and begin.

BLUEBERRY ARTWORK

Blueberries are certainly good for eating, but since they are such perfect little spheres, why not have your child create with them first—then she can munch her creation if she so desires!

1. Use toothpicks to stack the blueberries on to make blueberry people and animals.

2. Use an orange as a centerpiece—cut off a bottom slice to balance it—then stick blueberry-filled toothpicks in the orange to make various designs.

3. Make an edible glue of confectioner's sugar and milk or use peanut butter as glue and then create pictures and/or sculptures on a paper plate.

4. Give your child about 25 blueberries and a paper plate. Ask her to create a blueberry picture. It could be something as simple as a circle or as complex as a blueberry forest.

5. Give your child the same number of blueberries as you have for yourself and a paper plate. Make a design on your plate and have her duplicate the design. Then let her be the originator, if she wants.

BLUEBERRY PRINTS

You've made thumbprints with your child using ink before. Try making blueberry prints for fun. Merely take some overripe berries, put them on a white paper plate, and squash them. The juice from the berry will leave a stain in a very artistic way. Your child can arrange the blueberry "stains" ahead of time to make a certain design, or once the "stains" have been made, he can draw on additional features with a felt-tip marker to complete his blueberry print pictures.

SECOND WEEK

Some Things to Do When There's "Nothing" to Do

As much as children say they can't wait until school is out for the summer, there probably will be times when they say there is nothing to do. Perhaps it'll be on a rainy day when the pool is closed. Perhaps it'll be during the week that their best friends are away on vacation. Or it could simply be a time when they are tired of playing with the same things over and over again.

Before this happens, get prepared! If this book has been giving you some ideas, this temporary boredom might not ever happen to your children. But take some time now to plan ahead for the rest of summer. Have at your command some easy, summery activities to turn to when the occasion arises. Keep a list of places to go—for short walks, for bike hikes, for picnics, for an afternoon at a park, for a leisurely swim, for a rainy day alternative; projects to make; recipes to bake; and, of course, always have plenty of books on hand.

Below are some things to do with popsicle sticks, beach pebbles, and grocery bags, as these are easy things to collect during the summer that lend themselves nicely to crafts.

READINGS

Nothing To Do by Russell Hoban (Harper Junior)

Walter Possum can never find anything to do. Finally his dad gives him a magic stone. Any time Walter is at a loss for something to do, he is to rub it and the stone will come up with activities. Walter tries it, and it not only works for him but also helps him solve the same problem for his sister. Russell Hoban creates human-like animals with whom it is fun to associate and learn.

There's Nothing To Do by James Stevenson (Greenwillow Books)

MaryAnn and Louie tell Grandpa they hate being bored. Grandpa agrees and proceeds to tell them about a time when he was very bored. Grandpa spins another incredibly exaggerated and wonderful tale.

The Do-Something Day by Joe Lasker (Viking Press)

An energetic young boy wants to do something to help his family, but each person he approaches is too busy. He decides to run away. As he says goodbye to many of his friends he finds many things to do and learns a valuable lesson from his experiences.

RECITINGS

DON'T BE BORED
(Sung to "Working on the Railroad")

I've been sitting on these front steps
All the livelong day—
I've been sitting on these front steps
Just to pass the time away;
You'd think I'd get up and do something,
Rise up—find things to do;
You'd think I'd get up and do something,
But I don't have a clue.

You could bake a cake,
Muffins you could make,
Cookies you could take
When you go away.
You could pack a lunch,
With grapes by the bunch,
Let's get cooking right away.

Come on in the kitchen with _____,
Come on in the kitchen today,
Come on in the kitchen with _____,
You don't have to be bored today.

You could ride your bike,
Take a nice long hike,
Find an outdoor sport that you might like;
You could climb a tree,
A game of tag for three,
Being happy is the key.

Come out to the outside with _____,
Come out to the outside today,
Come out to the outside with _____,
You don't have to be bored today.

(Supply an appropriate name in the blanks.)

BORED, BORED, BORED
(Sung to "Row, Row, Row Your Boat")

Bored, bored, bored to tears
With nothing fun to do.
I can't think of anything great—
How about you?

RECIPES

YOGURT POPSICLES

1. Blend together 1 cup flavored yogurt, $\frac{1}{2}$ cup sliced fruit, 1 teaspoon vanilla, and 1 cup fruit juice or fruit chunks.
2. Pour into small paper cups.
3. Freeze. When mixture is half-frozen, put a popsicle stick or plastic spoon in each cup. Continue freezing.
4. To serve, turn each cup upside-down and run hot water over until the popsicle slips out, or peel the paper cup off the popsicle.

   Makes 4-5 small popsicles.

CREATE YOUR OWN POPSICLES

1. Blend together 1 cup cut-up or crushed fruit, 1 cup juice, and 1 cup water.
2. Pour into small paper cups.

   Follow steps 3 and 4 for the above recipe.

   Some ideas for combinations to use: grape, apple, orange, pineapple, cranberry juices; crushed fresh berries mixed with water.

   Other homemade popsicle ideas: yogurt with honey; pudding thinned down with milk; cider; or lemonade.

ACTIVITIES

POPSICLE STICK IDEAS

Set aside a container for all saved popsicle sticks—keep a running supply handy for when the mood strikes for a crafty project.

Give your child crayons, paints, felt markers, or stain to color the sticks and let his imagination take over. Glue them around the sides of orange juice cans to make pencil holders or flower vases; combine them to resemble rafts or boats and then set sail in the bathtub or down a nearby brook; make them into picture frames inside which your child can draw a picture or put a photograph; staple old greeting cards or cut-out pictures onto a stick and make puppets; or glue them crisscrossed in a square to make a trivet.

BEACH PEBBLE IDEAS

Whether you collect pebbles at the beach or in your own back yard, try to get a great variety of shapes, colors, and sizes to make the creative possibilities limitless.

Gather up the following supplies: pebbles, epoxy glue, marking pens or acrylic paints and brushes, scraps of material, and various odds and ends for adding details.

Now your child can create! He can turn these assorted items into something: a person; any type of familiar animal like a pig, a cow, a cat; a bus or car; a shoe; a plate or even a whole place setting for a meal or any type of appropriate food.

GROCERY BAG IDEAS

There always seems to be an endless supply of grocery bags, so why not use them creatively? Just for starters: let your child make hats or masks out of them, use them for collecting (give directions such as, "Find 5 orange things in the house that you can put in your bag"), take them on nature walks, have bag races in which participants must put both feet in the bag and jump to their destination, or decorate them and use them as wrapping paper.

THIRD WEEK

Creating Tall Tales

Have you ever heard your child say something like the following: "I love strawberries so much I ate a hundred million for breakfast" or "I'm so strong I picked up our whole house and carried it across the street"? Children are great tall tale–tellers. They are masters of exaggeration. Sometimes they get so involved in their fabricated stories they almost believe they are true. Tall tales are symbolic of the American way, as a flip through any magazine's advertisements will attest—"The world's best spaghetti sauce . . ." "The world's best-selling car . . . ." We are a country of the biggest, greatest, best, and tallest. Thus, many of our legendary stories reflect this. We have superheroes by the dozens who have supernatural powers and can do incredible things. Children feel a sense of power when relating to these extraordinary characters; and in a world where they might be made to feel small in comparison to their surroundings, this sense of power is important. Play along with your child's tall tales and be a part of this imaginary world where he is in charge for awhile.

READINGS

Cloudy with a Chance of Meatballs by Judi Barrett (Macmillan; pb Aladdin)

There are no food stores in Chewandswallow. People there don't need any because all the food that is ever needed is supplied three times each day by the weather! Life is fine until one day when the weather becomes undependable. Giant meatballs fall and damage houses. A tomato tornado strikes, leaving seeds and pulp everywhere. Something has to be done if the townspeople are to survive.

Paul Bunyan by Steven Kellogg (William Morrow & Co.)

This classic American tall tale is wonderfully re-told and illustrated by Steven Kellogg. Each page is brimming with stories as well as pictures of the things for which Paul Bunyan is famous.

McBroom and the Beanstalk by Sid Fleischman (Atlantic Little)

This tall tale about the McBroom family involves a bean seed which grows into a wildcat vine and proceeds to destroy anything in its way. This is just one of the many fantastic tall tales that involve the McBroom family that has delighted readers for years.

RECITINGS

MY DREAM
(Sung to "Looby Loo")
Here we go looby loo,
Here we go looby light,
Here we go looby loo,
All on a Saturday night.

I had a dream last night
That gave me quite a fright.
I should not tell—
I fear that spell—
Oh well, I guess I might.

While swimming in a lake,
A deep breath I did take,
I swam for days,
Went quite a ways,
More air I did not take.

Some hungry sharks I met—
I thought, "I'm dead, I bet."
They looked at me
And turned to flee,
I thought I was all set.

But then a shadow came.
It asked me for my name.
I could not see
What talked to me;
I answered just the same.

A witch then laughed and yelled
As she cast an evil spell,
1-2-3,
A frog I'd be,
If ever I did tell.

I told, but I'm okay—
My dream has gone away,
The witch was wrong,
She is long gone,
And I am here to stay.

But things don't feel all right,
I've lost my appetite,
I long for flies,
I realize,
"Croak!"—her spell was right!

Skunk followed her to the ice cream store;
Kids scattered from left to right.

Jenna walked right up and ordered a cone,
Ordered a cone, ordered a cone—
Jenna walked right up and ordered a cone;
Skunk asked to have a bite.

Kids watched as Skunk took his first taste,
His first taste, his first taste—
Kids watched as Skunk took his first taste,
To see what he might do.

Skunk paused, then turned as if to spray,
As if to spray, as if to spray—
Skunk paused, then turned as if to spray,
And then he turned to you.

He sprayed his scent directly at you,
Directly at you, directly at you—
He sprayed his scent directly at you,
But the shock was still to come.

The awful smell that you feared most,
You feared most, you feared most—
The awful smell that you feared most
Was tutti-frutti bubble gum!

RECIPES

JENNA HAD A LITTLE SKUNK
(Sung to "Mary Had a Little Lamb")

Jenna had a little skunk,
Little skunk, little skunk—
Jenna had a little skunk;
It was her favorite pet.

And everywhere that Jenna went,
Jenna went, Jenna went—
Everywhere that Jenna went,
Skunk scared off those they met.

Skunk followed her to the ice cream store,
The ice cream store, the ice cream store—

VERSATILE MEATBALLS

This recipe will make 3 dozen meatballs. There are many different ways to use them: in addition to the obvious pasta meals, or in soups, stews, sandwiches, and pizzas, have fun making people, animals, and other objects out of them. For example, to make a person, use two meatballs, grated carrot or cheese for hair, uncooked spaghetti for arms and legs, and tiny pieces of vegetables for facial features.

1. Mix together 1 pound of beef (or ground turkey), 1 egg, ½ cup fine bread crumbs, ¼ teaspoon pa-

prika, 1 tablespoon Worcestershire sauce, 1 tablespoon prepared mustard, and 1 tablespoon ketchup.

2. Shape into ½-inch diameter balls and arrange in a circular 9- or 10-inch glass pie plate if you want to microwave them, or in a baking pan for the oven.

3. Microwave: Cover with waxed paper and microwave at high for 6 to 8 minutes, rotating the dish ¼ turn after 3 minutes.

Conventional oven: Bake for 20-30 minutes at 350 degrees.

Meatballs may be frozen for later use.

THE BEST PIZZA IN THE WHOLE WIDE WORLD

To make your own pizza dough:

1. Combine 1 pound all-purpose flour (about 3¾ cups), 1 tablespoon yeast, 1 teaspoon salt, and ½ teaspoon sugar.

2. Add 1 tablespoon vegetable oil and 1 cup lukewarm water.

3. Mix together all ingredients.

4. Knead by hand for 3 minutes; shape; put in a bowl; cover and let rise until double in volume (about 1 hour).

5. Punch down; divide into 2 equal pieces; shape into round balls.

6. Let the dough rest for 4 minutes. Roll out into 12-inch diameter pizzas.

7. Put dough on lightly greased pizza pan (non-stick vegetable cooking spray is recommended).

8. Let dough rise for 10-15 minutes.

9. Preheat oven to 500 degrees.

10. Cover the crust with 1 cup spaghetti sauce; season with oregano, garlic powder, and salt to taste. Cover the pizza with ¼ pound thin-sliced

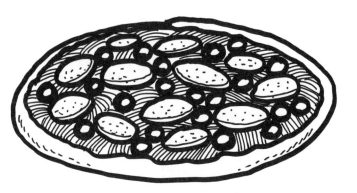

mozzarella cheese, and any other things you like (fried peppers and mushrooms, ham, pepperoni, sausage, ground cooked hamburger, or turkey); then dust with grated Parmesan cheese.

11. Bake 12-13 minutes.

You can freeze the pizza before cooking—put directly in the freezer until chilled; then cover with freezer wrap (with or without the pan) and leave in the freezer until ready to be used.

To cook frozen pizza, unwrap it, replace it on the pan, and bake in a preheated 350-degree oven until the cheese is melted and the crust is browned—about 30 minutes.

ACTIVITIES

TALL TALE PLAY

Make up some simple beginnings to some stories and together with your child create some tall tales. Here are several examples to get you thinking:

"Mommy and I were getting groceries last Saturday. We had just turned the corner to walk down the next aisle when we saw . . ."

"Daddy and I were going fishing last Sunday. We had only thrown our lines in for a few minutes when . . ."

WALKING TALL TALES

After you've created your own tall tales, take a long strip of adding machine tape about 3 inches wide. Write down one of your stories. Mount it on strips of black construction paper, add black legs and feet, and hang it up on a bulletin board, door, or wall.

TALL TALE RISERS

Make up a tall story to tell to your child. Instruct him that each time he hears you say something that is exaggerated he must rise up higher than he was. Have him start sitting on the floor or on a bottom stair and have him get higher each time. For instance, as you say something like, "Once there was a 215-year-old man . . . who had a farm. He could grow tomatoes as big as a beanbag chair . . .," he would progress from sitting on the floor to kneeling, standing, standing on a chair, and standing on the table.

FOURTH WEEK

You Make Me Laugh

Imagine yourself deadlocked in an argument with your spouse. Neither of you is willing to compromise or back down. If only you could think of something funny to say to break the silence, it might help both of you unwind gracefully. A good sense of humor can not only make life more pleasant, but it can also rescue you from some pretty desperate situations. Children generally tend to be so uninhibited and honest that experimenting with jokes comes naturally and is self-satisfying. At first they may not quite comprehend some of the subtleties and double meanings that make jokes funny, but once they catch on, watch out! Be prepared to hear one or two jokes repeated continuously for weeks. (And you must respond with the same enthusiasm and curiosity as you did initially, each time you hear the joke!)

Encourage joke-telling. It's a great means of expression, verbal communication, improving memory skills, dramatic play, and developing self-confidence—to name just a few of the positive benefits. This chapter includes several books and activities to augment your child's repertoire (and save your sanity!):

READINGS

The Marigold Monster by M.C. Delaney (Unicorn Books)

Audrey loves telling jokes but has a hard time finding someone who will listen to and appreciate them. When she meets a monster who eats people who tell corny jokes, Audrey realizes that her jokes will either gain an audience for her or lose every-thing *of* her! This humorous book is a fun introduction to the joys of joke telling.

Noah Riddle by Ann Bishop (Albert Whitman & Co.)

The punning title alone will tell you what this book is about. This book, along with the author's other joke collections, are enjoyable beginning joke books. (Some of the other books are *Oh Riddlesticks, Riddle Raddle Fiddle Faddle,* and *Hey Riddle Riddle.*)

The Gigantic Joke Book by Joseph Rosenbloom (Sterling Publishing Co.)

This wonderful collection of jokes is 250 pages chock-full of every kind of joke you can imagine.

RECITINGS

A JOKE TO TELL
(Sung to "The Muffin Man)
Do you know a joke to tell,
A joke to tell, a joke to tell?
Do you know a joke to tell
To make me laugh real hard?

Oh, yes, I know a joke to tell,
A joke to tell, a joke to tell,
Oh, yes, I know a joke to tell
To make you laugh real hard.

Did you take a bath today,
A bath today, a bath today?
Did you take a bath today?
(Spoken) No. Is there one missing?

AUGUST: A Month of Cures for the Late Summer Doldrums

ORIGINALS

My three sons think jokes are fun,
They love to make up their own.
With their okay, I'll tell them today,
To tickle your funny bone.

Matthew's favorite goes like this . . .
What kind of germ do some people live in?
(*Germ*any)

Michael has decided to buy a Ford car instead of a
Ferrari when he grows up because Fords are more
af*ford*able.

One day when I told Kyle that I was counting on
him to help, he replied, "One, two, three . . ."

RECIPES

GIGGLE SOUP

Make up a batch of funny soup to serve for a silly
lunch. Use a chicken broth as a base and add cut-up
vegetables and alphabet noodles. Use the ABC noodles to spell funny sounds and funny words on
your spoons.

GIGGLE SANDWICHES

Think of some edible but silly combinations for
sandwiches and choose one that sounds appetizing
to you. Some combos might be: cream cheese,
shredded carrots, and raisins; peanut butter and
sprouts; peanut butter and banana; egg salad and
pickles; tuna fish with cashews and grapes; chicken
salad with mandarin oranges and almonds.

After making the sandwich, cut it into a great big
smile shape and eat.

ACTIVITIES

LAUGHING LIST

It is always good to have a list of things that make
your child laugh. You never know when you might
need to refer to it to give her a little boost. Brainstorm with your child as to what things make her
laugh, and write them down. To get started: Write
down her favorite jokes; some funny episodes in
her life that make her laugh when she thinks of
them; perhaps tickling . . .

"PICTURE" THESE JOKES

Have your child think of his favorite jokes and
illustrate them.

PEN PAL JOKE EXCHANGE

Have your child ask a friend to be his "joke" pen
pal. Then have them take turns writing letters that
contain jokes to each other. The pen pal can be
someone who lives nearby or far away.

"FUNNIES" SCRAPBOOK

Get a scrapbook in which your child can save
any comic strips that she really likes. You can find
them in children's magazines, newspapers, and
other written sources.

CHAPTER NINE

SEPTEMBER
A Month of Friendship and Support

Most children view September in a rather bittersweet way. They are sad that their summer freedoms are over, yet happy to be back with their friends in a regular routine. Children are able to handle the anxieties, pressures, and concerns that school sometimes creates with greater ease knowing that friends and family are behind them all the way.

This is an important month to show your support, give an added ounce of attention, and offer an extra measure of patience to your child. Be a true friend to your child through good times as well as bad, happy as well as sad, anxious as well as secure. If your child knows you are there for her no matter what the situation, you will have an open line of communication forever.

The activities in this chapter will give you ideas on how to support your child if she should have back-to-school concerns or some bad days. There are also some ideas of ways for her to show her appreciation of her friends, both young and old. The celebration of Grandparents' Day on the second Sunday of this month gives a great opportunity for you to focus on the love the senior generation has to give.

FIRST WEEK

Back-to-School Anxiety

There is a certain amount of anxiety associated with the first day of something new. Everyone has questions and reservations about that first day, whether he is a newly appointed executive facing his judgmental staff, a sixteen-year-old hired for her first job, or a four-year-old starting to nursery school. They all have the same concerns. "Will I know what to do? . . . Will I know where to go? . . . Will there be someone there to help me? . . . Will there be someone there who will like me?"

As a parent of a child facing a new teacher/classroom/classmates, you can do many things to help ease this anxiety. The books and projects offered below will open up an opportunity for your child to discuss any of the concerns he may be feeling. Talking about it and preparing as much as possible are your two best preventive "medicines" against an anxiety attack.

READINGS

Will I Have a Friend? by Miriam Cohen (Macmillan; pb Aladdin Books)

As Jim and his daddy walk to school on Jim's very first day, Jim's thoughts are preoccupied by one overpowering question: "Will I have a friend at school?" Jim observes all kinds of exciting activities going on, but rather than participate he is more concerned with finding a friend. When he finally stops searching, he finds his friend resting right next to him.

Will I Have a Friend? is the first of a three-part series called the "School Survival Set," including *Best Friends* and *The New Teacher.* Simply and warmly, they all address issues that are of paramount importance to young children as they grow up.

That Dreadful Day by James Stevenson (Greenwillow Books)

Mary Ann and Louie come home from their first day of school feeling very displeased. They don't think they will go back to school tomorrow. When Grandpa tells them that the first day is always hard, he continues to tell them about his "tall tale" first-day experiences. This is another super exaggeration by James Stevenson.

I Don't Want to Go to School by Elizabeth Bram (Greenwillow Books)

It is Jennifer's first day of kindergarten and she doesn't want to go. Fortunately her understanding and patient mother eases her into going, because once she gets there she finds out that she loves it.

RECITINGS

SKIP TO MY SCHOOL
(Sung to "Skip to My Lou")
Skip, skip, skip to my school,
Skip, skip, skip to my school,
Skip, skip, skip to my school,
Skip to my school this morning.

Friends to meet at my school,
Friends to meet at my school,
Friends to meet at my school,
Skip to my school this morning.

A teacher who's sweet at my school,
A teacher who's sweet at my school,
A teacher who's sweet at my school,
Skip to my school this morning.

Books to read at my school, *etc.*

So many treats at my school, *etc.*

I'm in the lead to my school,
I'm in the lead to my school,
I'm in the lead to my school,
I can't wait for school this morning!

SCHOOL BEGINS
(Sung to "London Bridge")
School begins in one more day,
One more day, one more day.
School begins in one more day,
I'm so nervous.

New teachers' rules I must obey,
Must obey, must obey.
New teachers' rules I must obey,
I'm so nervous.

New kids to meet—what do I say?
What do I say? What do I say?
New kids to meet—what do I say?
I'm so nervous.

I don't want to go, so I'll run away,
I'll run away, I'll run away.
I don't want to go, so I'll run away,
I'm so nervous.

But there will be new games to play,
Games to play, games to play.
There will be new games to play,
I'm not quite so nervous.

And in art class we'll work with paint and clay,
Paint and clay, paint and clay.
In art class we'll work with paint and clay,
I'm not quite so nervous.

Maybe I'll like it and want to stay,
Want to stay, want to stay.
Maybe I'll like it and want to stay,
I'm not quite so nervous.

School can really be okay,
Be okay, be okay.
School can really be okay—
I'm not nervous!

RECIPES

AN APPLE FOR THE TEACHER AND CLASS
Whether this snack is brought to school on the first day to share with the whole class or as a special treat for the teacher, or is prepared for your family at home, it is fun and delicious and opens the opportunity to talk about school and snacks and teachers.

1. Take one apple and poke small holes in it with a fork.
2. Push thin pretzel sticks or sesame sticks into the holes (or use toothpicks, if you feel your child will handle them safely).

3. At the other end of each stick push one of the following: grapes, blueberries, strawberries, pineapple chunks, and/or other fruit pieces and cheese cubes. If you'd rather make a vegetable treat attach cherry tomatoes, olives, cucumber rounds, celery slices, or carrot slices to the toothpicks.

DRIED APPLE RINGS

This is another fun snack to make to take to school as a treat.

1. Peel an apple and remove the core. Slice in rings.
2. Place them on a lightly greased cookie sheet.
3. Dry them in an electric oven at low or warm temperature; in a gas oven the pilot light is sufficient.
4. Drying takes 6 to 9 hours, making this a good overnight project.
5. The size of your apple slices and your oven temperature are variables you will have to experiment with. The apples need not be dried to a crisp. Store them in an airtight container. They will last several weeks at room temperature.

ACTIVITIES

APPLE BOOK ABOUT YOU

This project may help your child feel more comfortable as she plans and creates a book about herself to give to her teacher. Through this book she will help her teacher get to know her better and at the same time she will be preparing something special and personal to make that first day less intimidating. Bringing something from home often bridges the gap between home and school and makes the transition easier.

1. Cut out a cover from construction paper and several inside pages in the shape of an apple.
2. Let your child decorate the cover and title the book as she wishes.
3. Use the inside pages to write whatever your child wants her teacher to know about her. Some suggestions: her name, brothers and sisters, pets, friends, hobbies, favorite sports, what she wants to learn this year.
4. Staple the pages all together.

SHOW AND TELL

Undoubtedly Show and Tell will be a prominent part of your child's school year. Help prepare her gently for this by talking about some of her favorite things that she might want to show to her friends at school. Perhaps she might even want you to write down a list of some of these things for her to refer to later on in the year. Ask her what it is that she likes about these things and encourage her to talk freely.

Role-play Show and Tell as well as any other part of school that your child may wish to act out. This will also encourage discussions about any fears and concerns she may be feeling about school.

PLAN AHEAD

Find out what some of your child's main concerns are and address them.

If she is worried about riding on the bus, take her to the lot where the buses are parked and let her see one. If you should be fortunate enough to see someone working there, ask if you could just step inside the bus to let your child sit in one of the seats. This might ease her mind about the "big steps" and give her a little more confidence on that first day.

If she is concerned about finding her classroom, go to the school one day before school starts and walk around the school to help her locate not only her classroom but even the cafeteria, gym, and bathrooms, and walk her through what she wants to know. Usually at least a janitor, if not the principal, teachers, and secretaries, will be there preparing for the opening of school several weeks early.

If your child is concerned about not knowing who will be in her class, try to find out at least one name of a classmate-to-be and invite that child over to play some afternoon.

You can do plenty to help ease your child's fears without being intrusive.

SECOND WEEK

Grandparents—Those Very Special People

There is an expression that reads, "If I had known grandchildren were so much fun, I'd have had them first!" Although comical and a bit satirical, this statement certainly brings up a good point. A person's capacity for love reaches new heights when he experiences grandparenthood. What is it that makes grandparenthood so rewarding and fulfilling? Grandparenthood is essentially all the love and joys of parenting minus the headaches and responsibilities. Grandparents can give as freely and as generously as they wish without the fear of overindulging or spoiling the children. Mom and Dad need to be somewhat more conservative. Time and experience have taught the senior generation to be more relaxed, patient, and accepting with children. And in return for their "grand parenting," grandparents win the devoted and tender love of their grandchildren.

Grandparents' Day is observed nationally on the first Sunday after Labor Day. It is a day set aside to show appreciation for the seniors in your lives. Whether your children's grandparents are nearby or live far away, whether your children have real grandparents or "honorary" ones, spend some time planning a notable day for these people who mean so much to and do so much for your children.

READINGS

A Special Trade by Sally Wittman (Harper Junior Books)

Nelly and Bartholomew have such a deep friendship that even time can't change it. From the time Nelly is a little baby they spend hours enjoying each other's company. As the years pass they find the only things that change are the roles they play. This warm, touching book beautifully illustrates an ageless love between young and old.

Now One Foot, Now the Other by Tomie de Paola (G.P. Putnam's Sons)

Bobby's best friend is his grandfather, Bob. They are inseparable. One day Bob has a stroke and Bobby is told Bob will never be the same again. Bobby is scared at first, but he conquers his fear through love, and in the process conquers a great deal more for Bob.

Special Friends by Terry Berger (Julian Messner)

A little girl tells of her very special friendship with

her "Aunt" Rosie. The treasured afternoons they spend together are filled with warm and caring activities and conversations. The black and white photographs enhance this already beautiful story that shows the tenderness of love shared between young and old.

RECITINGS

OH, DEAR GRANDMA
(Sung to "Oh, Susannah")

She comes from her warm kitchen with home
    cooking from her place,
She comes over to my house with a smile upon
    her face.
We play all day the times she comes,
Read books and have such fun,
We sing and draw and paint and bake,
Take walks out in the sun.

Oh, dear Grandma,
I love you so, you see.
The time we spend together
Is so wonderful for me.

MY GRANDFATHER
(Sung to "This Old Man")

My grandfather taught me one,
He taught me how to have some fun,
Chorus:
With a knick-knack-patty-whack,
Look into his eyes—
My grandfather is very wise.

My grandfather taught me two,
He taught me that a friend is true,
(Chorus)

My grandfather taught me three,
He taught me to listen carefully,
(Chorus)

My grandfather taught me four,
He taught me skills but so much more,
(Chorus)

My grandfather taught me five,
He taught me how to be really alive,
(Chorus)

RECIPES

CONGO BARS

    This family recipe always reminds me of my own children's "grand"mother, my mom!

1. Preheat oven to 350 degrees.
2. Mix together $2\frac{1}{4}$ cups brown sugar (1 pound), $\frac{2}{3}$ cup melted margarine, and 3 eggs in a bowl.
3. Add $2\frac{3}{4}$ cups sifted flour, $\frac{1}{2}$ teaspoon salt, and $2\frac{1}{2}$ teaspoons baking powder all together.
4. Mix in 1 teaspoon vanilla, 1 cup chopped walnuts, and 1 cup chocolate bits.
5. Spread in a 9-by-13-inch greased pan and bake for about 25 minutes.
6. After cooling, cut into brownie-size squares.

    Makes about $2\frac{1}{2}$ dozen.

SAVORY GRANDPARENTS' TEA

    A tasty drink to serve with Congo Bars.

1. Boil 6 cups of water in a kettle.
2. Cut 1 orange and 1 lemon into quarters and put 2 orange quarters and 2 lemon quarters into a teapot.
3. Add 1 cranberry, raspberry, or orange herbal tea bag, 1 cinnamon stick, and 1 whole clove in the teapot.
4. Pour the boiling water into the teapot. Cover the pot and let the mixture heat for 3 minutes. Remove the cover and press down on the orange and lemon quarters with a wooden spoon. Stir the mixture well. Remove the tea bag and the other ingredients.
5. Fill 4 tea cups with the freshly brewed tea. Serve with the extra orange and lemon quarters.

    Makes 4-6 cups.

ACTIVITIES

Plan a little party when your child can spend time treating his grandparents.

GRANDSNACKS

Help your child think of some of his grandparents' favorite snacks and prepare one or two of them. The two recipes given above might be appropriate. Pack the food up in a basket lined with handsome napkins and decorated with ribbons and bows.

LET ME ENTERTAIN YOU

Perhaps your child can play a game of cards with her grandparents as a treat for them. Or she might stage a puppet show, play a song on a musical instrument that you play, sing a song, or perform some dance or acrobatic feat. Whatever she chooses, her grandparents will be thrilled to be the recipients of her time and thoughtfulness.

FAMILY INTERVIEW

If it would be appropriate and viewed as something exciting and rewarding to all involved, plan an interviewing session between grandparent and grandchild. What better way for a child to learn more about his grandparents and the way in which they grew up and came to be what they are today? Tailor it to what is comfortable for those involved. You may wish to tape-record the interview so that it can be as spontaneous as possible. If this is too inhibiting, take notes.

Plan ahead of time what questions will be asked. Some general thoughts and possible suggestions follow to help you and your child organize your thoughts.

■ Family—Who were all the members of your family; what were mealtimes like; did you have big parties for holidays?

■ Friends—Who were your good friends; what did you do together?

■ Vacations—Where did you go; how did you get there; did you stay in a hotel?

■ Holidays—Favorites; traditions?

■ Food—Favorites?

■ Clothes—What were the styles?

■ School—Where did you go; who were your favorite teachers; what did you like or dislike about school; what was your favorite subject?

■ Entertainment—What kinds; books; TV; radio?

■ Pets—Did you have any; what were their names?

■ Dating and marriage—How did you meet; where did you go out when dating; what did you do?

■ Work—What did you do to earn a living; did you ever change jobs?

■ Raising my mom/dad—What was my mom/dad like as a baby? Did he or she ever get in trouble? What was the funniest thing he or she did as a child?

THIRD WEEK

Bad Days Happen to Everyone

Bad things happen to everyone occasionally. Oversleeping and being late for an appointment, burning a gourmet meal you've painstakingly planned for dinner guests, waking up to torrential rains while vacationing, or being caught in rush-hour traffic can disarm even the most positive optimist. But have you ever had a day when from dawn till dusk you experience nothing but bad things? It takes a good sense of humor and careful insight to get through this type of day with a smile.

Children have bad days, too. To adults, the obstacles children face might seem insignificant and silly, but to that child, those obstacles are major. It's comforting for children to know that everyone has bad days. And it's helpful if you can ease their frustration by offering some concrete things to do. Below are some suggestions on what to do when one of those days strikes.

READINGS

Alexander and the Terrible, Horrible, No Good, Very Bad Day by Judith Viorst (Macmillan; pb Aladdin Books)

When Alexander wakes up with gum in his hair he can tell it's going to be a bad day. And he is right! His mother forgets to give him dessert with his lunch; when he goes to the dentist for a check-up, he has a cavity; he gets soap in his eyes while taking a bath; his night light burns out—and those are only a few of the things that go wrong.

This book is a great comfort for all children to relate to when they have a bad day.

Could Be Worse by James Stevenson (Greenwillow Books)

Mary Ann and Louie think that life for Grandpa must be pretty boring. He never seems to say anything interesting. But when Grandpa overhears this conversation he weaves a tale of woes that keep getting worse and worse.

Herbie's Troubles by Carol Chapman (E.P. Dutton)

Herbie's troubles all begin when he meets Jimmy John. Jimmy goes out of his way every day to cause trouble for Herbie. Herbie gets advice from his friends, but nothing works until Herbie figures out his own way to handle his problems.

RECITINGS

BAH, BAH, HUMBUG
(Sung to "Baa, Baa, Black Sheep")
Bah, bah, humbug,
What a crummy day.
It's so bad
I think I'll run away.

First I slept late,
Then I tripped over my cat.
My banana was rotten,
And my pancakes were too flat.

Baa, baa, humbug,
What a crummy day.
It's so bad
I think I'll run away.

School was a disaster,
My teacher yelled at me.
At recess I tripped
Over a big root of a tree.

Bah, bah, humbug,
What a crummy day.
It's so bad
I think I'll run away.

When I got home,
The door was locked tight.
I stayed at my friend's
And we got into a fight.

Bah, bah, humbug,
What a crummy day.
It's so bad
I think I'll run away.

But when the day was over,
My parents said to me,
"Everyone has days like this,"
Then gave me a big squeeze.

Bah, bah, humbug,
What a crummy day.
It wasn't all that bad,
I think I want to stay.

THE CRANKPOT
(Sung to "I'm a Little Teapot")

I'm a little crankpot, raging mad,
Today is the worst day I've ever had.
When I get so angry, it's really bad,
Please tickle me till I am glad.

SURPRISE CUPCAKES

These are great to have on hand (keep some in the freezer) for a surprise "pick-me-up" to cheer up your sad little one when he is having a bad day.

1. Preheat oven to 350 degrees.
2. Beat together $1\frac{1}{2}$ cups flour, 1 cup sugar, $\frac{1}{4}$ cup cocoa, 1 teaspoon baking soda, 1 teaspoon vanilla, $\frac{1}{2}$ teaspoon salt, 1 cup water, $\frac{1}{3}$ cup vegetable oil, and 1 tablespoon vinegar (or if you'd prefer, prepare any flavor layer cake mix as directed on the package).
3. In another bowl, beat together 8 ounces of softened cream cheese, 1 egg, $\frac{1}{3}$ cup sugar, and $\frac{1}{2}$ cup chocolate bits.
4. In greased cupcake tins, put 2 tablespoons of batter #1, then 1 tablespoon of batter #2, and sprinkle with chopped walnuts.
5. Bake for 30 minutes.
   Makes 24 cupcakes.

SNICKERDOODLES

The name alone can cheer up a sad face!

1. Preheat oven to 375 degrees.
2. Beat $\frac{3}{4}$ cup margarine and 1 cup sugar.
3. Add 2 eggs, $\frac{3}{4}$ cup milk, 2 teaspoons baking powder, and $2\frac{1}{2}$ cups flour.
4. Drop by teaspoonfuls onto greased cookie sheet.
5. Mix together $\frac{1}{4}$ cup sugar and 1 teaspoon nutmeg. Sprinkle cookies with sugar/nutmeg mixture. Put one raisin in the middle of each cookie.
6. Bake for 10 minutes.

ACTIVITIES

SMILE LIST

Make a list of things that make your child smile. It's best to be prepared for when a bad day strikes. So confer with your child ahead of time and have this list on hand to refer to when you need it.

■ Music—Is there a song that always makes your child happy when you sing it, or play it for him or with him?

■ People—Are there certain people that your child likes to be with or talk to who can cheer him up?

■ Places to go—Are there certain places in your own house, or places that you can walk to, or places that you can take your child that always make him feel happy?

■ Books—Are there any particular books that he loves that make him feel good and happy when you read them to him?

■ Food—Is there a special treat that he loves to eat that makes him feel better? (Don't overuse this, or you may end up with even "bigger" problems!)

■ Miscellaneous—List any other things that make him feel good and happy—perhaps coloring, artwork, exercising, or riding his bike.

BODY PAINTING

Doing something a little crazy can often make us feel better. This activity can be as creative and silly as you want it to be.

1. Have your child put on old clothes and get out some tempera paints, make-up, or face paints.
2. Put cold cream on her skin.
3. Begin painting—try a smiling elbow, a flowered ankle, a knee-monster, arm stripes, or a nose-butterfly.
4. When you are finished and she is feeling happier, wash with soap and water.

PUNCHING BAG

Make a simple punching bag out of a balloon tied to a string. Suspend it from the ceiling and let your child "punch" out his sad feelings.

FOURTH WEEK

Learning about Friends by Being One

If you are fortunate enough to have a best friend, you know how precious that person is to you. Time shared with that person is great no matter what you do. A simple walk, a class taken together, or a playgroup with your children all seem even richer when shared with your best friend. Whether you talk about aerobics, politics, recipes, or the kids, you feel stimulated and fulfilled. There are never any feelings of jealousy or revenge, only love and respect for each other. No matter what happens you know you will always be there for each other.

We, as parents, are our children's first playmates and friends. Time spent together is precious and fulfilling. But we should not be our children's only friends. Friends of similar ages offer much to each other as they interact and learn together. The activities and books mentioned below deal with friends and offer different things to do with and for one's best friend. As you do some of these projects, help your child to appreciate just how fantastic friends are.

READINGS

Best Friends for Frances by Russell Hoban (Harper & Row)

Albert is Frances's very good friend. But when he excludes her from an outing she turns to her pesky little sister, Gloria. She finds that she can have a great time with Gloria, too. When she and Albert resolve their differences Frances ends up with two best friends, Albert and Gloria.

Frog and Toad Are Friends by Arnold Lobel (Harper & Row)

Frog and Toad are the best of friends. This book has five little chapters—each one telling about another one of their exciting adventures. There are several other Frog and Toad books telling more of their heartwarming adventures.

We Are Best Friends by Aliki (Greenwillow)

When Peter tells Robert he is moving, Robert feels Peter can't move because they are best friends. But Peter moves anyway. Robert spends some lonely and angry times missing Peter until he meets Will. Then he comes to understand that having a new friend doesn't take away the friendship he already has with his old friend.

Aliki not only touches the subject of friendships but also simply handles the heartbreak of missing a dear friend who moves away.

RECITINGS

JACK AND BILL
(Sung to "Jack and Jill")

Jack and Bill
Are friends until
The sun no longer rises;
They're so tight,
They seldom fight,
And love to share surprises.

Jack and Bill
Are friends until
The stars fall from the sky;
They go everywhere,
They like to share,
And they see eye to eye.

123

THREE BEST FRIENDS
(Sung to "Three Blind Mice")

Three best friends, three best friends,
See how they play, see how they play,
They all run after the soccer ball,
They help each other if one should fall,
Did you ever see such a threesome all
Of three best friends?

RECIPES

FRIENDSHIP COOKIES

These are such super cookies, your child will want to share them with his best friend.

1. Preheat oven to 375 degrees.
2. Combine ³/₄ cup wheat germ, ³/₄ cup flour, ¹/₄ cup semi-sweet chocolate pieces, ¹/₄ cup flaked coconut, ¹/₄ cup uncooked quick oats, 1 teaspoon baking powder, and ¹/₂ teaspoon salt. Stir well to blend.
3. Cream ¹/₂ cup softened margarine and ¹/₈ cup packed brown sugar and ¹/₈ cup sugar thoroughly. Beat in 1 egg and ³/₄ teaspoon vanilla.
4. Add blended dry ingredients to creamed mixture. Blend well.
5. Place batter by heaping teaspoonfuls onto greased baking sheets, about 6 inches apart. Flatten with a spatula.
6. Bake for 8 minutes until cookies are golden brown and centers are firm.
7. Cool on pan for 2 minutes. Remove from pan. Cool on rack.

  Makes 3 dozen cookies.

SHARE A SHAKE

Blend the following ingredients in the blender to make a milkshake, and let your child share it with a friend.

■ Orange Milk Shake—1 cup orange juice, ¹/₄ cup dry milk, ¹/₄ teaspoon vanilla, and 1 cracked ice cube

■ Banana Milk Shake—1 ripe banana, 1 cup milk, ¹/₄ teaspoon vanilla, and 1 cracked ice cube

■ Grape Milk Shake—¹/₂ cup milk, 3 ounces frozen grape juice concentrate. Blend in blender, then add 1 cup vanilla ice cream. Blend for 20 seconds more.

FRIENDSHIP CARE PACKAGE

Whether your child's friend lives next door or across town or has moved to California, have her send her a care package to let her know just how much she cares about her. Here are some suggestions as to what to include: a batch of Friendship Cookies (see recipe above); a tape of herself talking or singing; one of her favorite toys that she can loan her for a few days; a recent picture of herself (if the friend lives far away); a card that explains why she is sending this surprise package (see activities below); and a Fuzzy Animal (see activities below).

ACTIVITIES

CARE CARD

Get any paper and fold it into a card—whatever size your child wishes. Get a stamp pad and have her make thumbprints and fingerprints on the card in a design or picture. Use felt markers to add details. Make up appropriate sayings about friendship to add to the artwork. Some ideas borrowed from songs might be, "That's what friends are for," "Oh, you've got to have friends," "You've got a friend," or "You're a friend of mine."

FUZZY ANIMALS

These make great puppets or, if your child chooses to stuff them, cuddly stuffed animal friends.

1. Precut out of felt any animal shape your child wishes—make 2 pieces exactly the same.

2. Help with the stitching—if this is to be a puppet, remember to leave one side open for the hand to fit in. If this is to be a stuffed animal, stitch with the pieces inside out. Stitch as much as possible, leaving enough of an opening to turn it right side in and then stuff with cotton or other filler.

3. Then allow your child to add the "fuzzies" by gluing on any or all of the following items: yarn, cotton, pieces of carpet samples, various other colors and shapes of felt, discarded fur, or any other material scraps that would work.

STICKER SWAP

If your child's friend and she both like to collect stickers, they may wish to begin a sticker club in which they swap stickers that they have collected. They can keep them in a notebook or in envelopes and trade them at club meetings that they hold on certain days. (If the friend lives far away, they can send their stickers to each other.)

CHAPTER TEN

OCTOBER
A Chilling Month

October is chilling for children in some geographic areas because of the changes in the weather. Frosty mornings and crisp afternoons provide cool settings for outdoor play.

But October is chilling in another respect too. Halloween arrives at the end of this month, bringing ghostly, ghastly, and eerie images to scare a chill into every child. Handled

appropriately and carefully, these motifs will cause no harm. In fact a great deal of pleasure and fun can be had from the fear-inducing entertainment associated with Halloween. But be wary of the surfacing of certain childhood fears—including that of death—and be ready to handle them. Have a frightfully good time as you get ready for this chilling month.

FIRST WEEK

Enjoying Autumn's Beauty

Some may view autumn as a sad time of year, signifying the end of warm and enjoyable weather. But the season can be viewed in a different light. Autumn is full of brilliant oranges, flamboyant reds, vibrant purples, and warm yellows. It is a time of invigorating outdoor play, as children try to catch falling leaves before they touch the ground or hurdle into a newly raked pile of leaves. Make the most of this time of year with your child and capture some of the vitality of autumn.

READINGS

Leaf Magic by Margaret Mahy (J.M. Dent & Sons Ltd)

When Michael wishes for a dog of his own to play with and to run through the autumn woods with, he doesn't notice that the trees are listening. What he does notice is a big orange leaf that begins following him and continues to follow him for an entire day. Figuring that he must be under a spell, Michael seeks help. There is a wonderfully happy ending that will please all believers in magic.

Tale of Squirrel Nutkin by Beatrix Potter (Simon & Schuster, Inc.)

It is autumn—time for squirrels to gather nuts to get ready for winter. Nutkin, Twinkleberry, and their cousins travel daily to a nut-covered island laden with gifts for Old Mr. Brown, an owl who lives on this island. In return, he allows them to take as many nuts as they can carry. All transactions go smoothly, except that Nutkin's constant impertinence gets him in a great deal of trouble.

Down Come the Leaves by Henrietta Bancroft (Thomas Y. Crowell Co.)

In this joyful book about autumn the reader will learn many things about leaves—why they fall and change color, what the many different types are, and much more.

RECITINGS

FALLING, FALLING LITTLE LEAF
(Sung to "Twinkle, Twinkle, Little Star")
Falling, falling little leaf,
Do you feel a great relief?
Up so high all summer long,
Having to hang on so strong.

Now that fall has finally come,
You release and go on home,
Back to the ground so nice and low,
Where the wind will help you blow—

Blow until comfort you find;
Settle in a bed of pine,
Taking on a brand-new form,
Part of earth, so nice and warm.

Falling, falling little leaf,
Do you feel a great relief?

FALL LEAVES
(Sung to "Eensy Weensy Spider")

One orangey yellow fall leaf
Fell softly to the ground.
Down came some more
And circled it around.
Out came some children
To run around and play,
And they frolicked in the fall leaves
That bright fresh autumn day.

LEAF PILE SALAD

Make a "leaf pile" tossed salad with your child using the following ingredients: red leaf lettuce; red, green, and yellow peppers cut into leaf shapes; tomato wedges; and broccoli spears. Make a dressing using 2 tablespoons vinegar, 1/2 cup mayonnaise, 1/4 cup sugar, and 1 teaspoon onion salt. Blend well. Toss and serve.

RECIPES

ACTIVITIES

AUTUMN LEAF TOAST

This colorful art project is twice as nice because once your masterpiece is done, you can eat it.

1. Pour 1 tablespoon of milk into each of four paper cups.
2. Add one or two drops of food coloring to each cup—red, blue, yellow, and green. If you are uncomfortable using food coloring, experiment with various juices to obtain the colors you'd like. For example, use orange juice, cranberry juice, grape juice.
3. Take a piece of bread and cut it into a leaf shape.
4. Give your child a paintbrush and let him paint the "leaf" with various colors to make a fall leaf.
5. Put the "leaf" in the toaster, toast, then butter lightly, if desired.

LEAF RUBBINGS

Place a leaf under a smooth piece of paper. Have your child gently rub with the side of a crayon in the same direction across the leaf and around its outline. Let him do several leaves, perhaps making a design, perhaps cutting them out when they are done, or using them as decorations.

PRESERVED LEAVES

Help your child place a firm leaf between two pieces of waxed paper. Place the waxed paper on several layers of newspaper, cover with more newspaper, then press with a warm iron. Remove all the newspaper and he'll have a preserved leaf that he can hang in a window or use as a decoration.

LEAF PRINTS

Help your child coat one side of a leaf with thick one-color tempera paint by using a brayer or a homemade block printing dabber (rolled paper toweling will do fine). Gently lay the leaf, paint side down, on a piece of heavy paper, lift carefully, and repeat the process on other leaves. Use a variety of colors of paint and paper.

LEAF "CRITTERS"

Collect various-sized and -shaped leaves, seed pods, and/or sticks with your child. Have your child glue them to cardboard, add eyes, legs, and other features by drawing them in with a crayon or marker, and give her "critter" a name.

LEAF "FEELY BOARD"

Collect leaves, sticks, dried grass, pods, seeds, and pinecones. Glue 4 or 5 things you've collected on a piece of cardboard. Leave space between each one. Blindfold your child. Have her carefully touch and feel. What is on the board? Describe how each thing feels.

SECOND WEEK

Handling Childhood Fears

Fears are as common to growing children as skinned knees. Childhood fears, whether of monsters, darkness, being alone, sudden noises, doctors, baths, masks, strangers, or something else, are virtually unavoidable even for the most secure of children. Some of these fears may seem silly and insignificant to an adult, but to the child they are far from funny. Eventually your child will outgrow his fears as his experiences prove there is nothing to be afraid of. But in the meantime, there is much we can do to support, reassure, and comfort our frightened little ones.

Perhaps the most important thing to remember is that your child will never benefit from the phrase "There's nothing to be afraid of" unless you add to it, "Mommy and Daddy love you and we will always protect you from any real danger." Don't negate your child's fears by saying there's no such thing as monsters or whatever he is concerned about; rather respect his fear as being very real to him and help him deal with it. For example, if he is afraid of a monster in his closet, help him to come up with a solution to get rid of it. Talking about the fear as often as he needs to helps a great deal, too. Carefully plan and monitor the television shows, movies, and books your child is exposed to, previewing and prereading any questionably frightening ones.

With Halloween just around the corner, give a few extra moments of thought to your child's fears. Inventory his fears and plan ahead to be able to handle anything that might arise. The books and activities below may help your child to understand that he isn't the only one who is afraid at times.

READINGS

Harry and the Terrible Whatzit by Dick Gackenbach (Houghton Mifflin; pb Ticknor & Fields)

When Harry's mom insists on going down in the cellar to get a jar of pickles, he knows she'll never come back up, for there is something terrible down there. After waiting and waiting at the cellar door, he decides to go down himself. Someone has to do something. So Harry confronts his most dreaded fear out of his love for his mom and finds a hidden resource of bravery he never knew he had.

Through this clever book, Dick Gackenbach comforts children by showing that everyone has fears, and also gives some sound advice on how to handle them.

There's a Nightmare in My Closet by Mercer Mayer (Dial Press)

Mercer Mayer deals with a child's fear of the dark and bedtime in a sensitive and novel way.

Also available by the author on the subject of nighttime fears is *There's an Alligator under My Bed* (Dial Books for Young Readers).

Jim Meets the Thing by Miriam Cohen (Greenwillow Books)

When Jim watches The Thing on television he gets really scared. But the next day in school no one else is, and he feels ashamed that he is such a coward. But later on during the day Jim proves that he is much braver than all the rest of the kids in his class. This is just one of many perceptive books about Jim and his first-grade class.

RECITINGS

NIGHTTIME CHILLS
(Sung to "Jingle Bells")

Dashing through the dark,
Feeling not so very brave,
Through the dark I race,
Hoping my life to save.
Monsters hiding there,
Under the attic stairs,
Goblins waiting everywhere
To grab me by the hair.

Oh, nighttime chills
And monsters will
Scare you every day.
If you let them bother you,
They'll steal your fun away.

But you can win,
Face them and grin,
Just push your fears aside.
You are smarter than they are,
So you don't need to hide.

DID YOU EVER SEE A MONSTER?
(Sung to "Did You Ever See a Lassie?")

Did you ever see a monster,
A monster, a monster—
Did you ever see a monster
Who looked just like this?

His hair is bright red,
Curling 'round his square head.
Did you ever see a monster
Who looked just like that?

Did you ever see a monster,
A monster, a monster—
Did you ever see a monster
Who looked just like this?

Four eyes are all black,
Two face front, two face back.
Did you ever see a monster
Who looked just like that?

Did you ever see a monster,

A monster, a monster—
Did you ever see a monster
Who looked just like this?

Sharp teeth fill his mouth,
Facing north, east, and south.
Did you ever see a monster
Who looked just like that?

Did you ever see a monster,
A monster, a monster—
Did you ever see a monster
Who looked just like this?

He stands twelve feet high,
His eight arms touch the sky.
Did you ever see a monster
Who looked just like that?

RECIPES

MONSTER EGGS
Have all these ingredients available for your child to create his own monster; then let him eat it up.

1. Hard-boil some eggs.
2. Peel the eggs, cut a slice off the larger end of each so that they can stand up, and set them on a slice of tomato.
3. Have available and let your child create with the following ingredients: green and/or black olives, carrot sticks, pickles, radish, green beans, celery, paprika, or other spice to sprinkle on as hair, and any other vegetable that might lend itself to being a good monster-feature!
4. Use mayonnaise to stick the features onto the egg. (A toothpick or two might be needed to help stick some things on, but supervise the use of the toothpicks.)

MONSTER PIZZAS

Another fun way to be creative with food, then eat up your creation.

1. Toast English muffin halves and cover each half with pizza sauce.

2. Let your child make her monster face pizza with any of the following: olives, grated cheese, bits of meat, or vegetables.

3. Stick the pizza under the broiler for a few minutes, then let your child munch her monster.

ACTIVITIES

A MYRIAD OF MASKS

Masks can be very frightening things for children until they learn to separate reality from fantasy. They need to see the person underneath a mask to realize that it is only a mask and not the scary creature it appears to be. The more play and experience children have with masks, the less intimidated they will be when they encounter one. Below are several suggestions of masks one can make.

If you are looking for some illustrations or more ideas on mask making, try your library. One helpful book is *Mask Making* by Chester J. Alkema.

Paper Bag Masks

Why not use this readily available resource to make some easy masks? Before drawing on a face, place the paper bag over your child's head to see where it rests on her shoulders. Then mark where her eyes, nose, and mouth would be so that you can first cut those holes out. Once that is done, have your child create whatever she'd like.

Paper Plate Masks

A paper plate can be transformed into just about anything your child would like with a few crayons and a little creativity. If he wants to wear it after it is done, punch a hole on either side of the plate and tie yarn, ribbon, or string to each hole. Extend it out long enough to allow ample room to tie it around his head.

Yarn and Pipe Cleaner Masks

Various colors of yarn and pipe cleaners can make very clever and unusual masks. Take heavy paper (like poster board or corrugated cardboard) and cut it into a shape your child would like the mask to be. Then she can glue on yarn or pipe cleaners in whatever pattern she'd like—reshaping the yarn to fit her design easily.

Papier-Mâché Masks

This is rather involved, but worth the effort if you'd like to tackle it together.

First, make the homemade papier-mâché paste: Stir 1 1/2 cups of flour into 3 cups cold water; cook over low heat until the mixture thickens to a creamy paste. Add more water if the mixture gets too thick. Cool. Add a few drops of oil of peppermint. (Or you can use wallpaper paste—instructions are on the package.) Now assemble the mask, below.

1. Grease the bottom and sides of a pie pan or cake tin with petroleum jelly.

2. Cut newspaper or paper towels into strips—dip them into the paste you've made. Cover your pan with 2 layers.

3. Make eyes, noses, mouths, ears, wrinkles, and such by pasting on more strips or other materials like yarn, spools, or egg cartons.

4. Cover these pieces with 2 more layers of pasted strips.

5. Allow to dry for a day or so. When the papier-mâché is completely dry, pop the pie pan out, then paint and decorate the mask.

THIRD WEEK

Helping Your Child Grieve

Death is difficult for children to understand, yet it affects them, too. Everyone has his own personal way of grieving; there is no right or wrong way. Grieving in any form is necessary in the healing process. Whether your child's grief takes the form of anger, tears, guilt, despair, protest, or denial, it is his expression of love—his own way of saying, "I miss you." It's vital that you allow as much grieving time as your child needs. If he feels sad, assure him that it's all right to feel sad. Sadness is much like a pain one feels after an injury; at first the pain is intense, but with each passing day it diminishes. The sadness, too, will gradually diminish and eventually one will be able to think about the deceased without feeling so blue.

Sadness is just one of several natural reactions your child may feel after experiencing such a loss. There may be a period of eating and sleeping difficulties or a time when he might vacillate between anger and aggression. There may be a period of poor performance and a lack of concentration. Your child may feel a tremendous void in his life; he may need more physical comfort and affection. He may want more of everything. As a parent, try to recognize these signs as forms of grieving and be as compassionate, patient, and understanding as possible. There are several ways to help your child handle grief. Most important is to talk as much and as often about it as he wishes. He may experience a phase of denial, and talking about it over and over will help him cope with reality.

Respond to his natural curiosity, making sure to answer only what he wishes to know. When questions arise, answer them simply and directly. Don't offer more details than he is ready to handle. If you are unsure about what he is really asking, be sure to ask first, "Just what is it that you want to know?" to help clarify it.

Read simple stories about death. Animal stories are easier for children to relate to. Even if a particular book doesn't deal with the exact situation over which your child is grieving, the book will still be helpful because it will provide an opportunity for your child to ask questions that are concerning him.

This chapter is being offered in preparation for families whose children will, unfortunately, have to deal with the sadness of death. Inevitably we will all face the death of some of our loved ones, and although nothing can ever make it easy, after having read this chapter you may have a little more confidence in presenting this very difficult subject to your child.

READINGS

The Tenth Good Thing about Barney by Judith Viorst (Macmillan)

In an attempt to cope with the death of his cat, Barney, a young boy, makes a list of 10 good things he remembers about him. This way of remembering Barney acts in a positive way to console the boy and help him deal with his grief. This is a very tender and gentle story that will help young children identify with and deal with death.

The Accident by Carol Carrick (Seabury Press)

When Christopher's dog, Badger, gets killed by a car, he is angry with everyone. His hurt and pain are lessened when his dad helps him remember some of the wonderful things about Badger.

My Grandson, Lew by Charlotte Zolotow (Harper & Row)

Lewis misses his Grandpa late one night and wants to talk to his mom about him. As they share their loving memories of him they both lessen their loneliness and pain.

Nanna Upstairs and Nanna Downstairs by Tomie de Paola (Putnam)

Every Sunday afternoon Tommy and his family visit his grandmother and his great-grandmother. He loves them very much and enjoys being with them. When they die he learns about a new way of loving them—through happy memories.

RECITINGS

COME HUG ME, SWEETHEART
(Sung to "Rockabye, Baby")

Come hug me, sweetheart, tears in your eyes,
When someone dies, it's hard not to cry,
Your heart aches so, you hurt everywhere,
But happy memories will always be there.

CRY, MY SWEETHEART
(Sung to "Hush, Little Baby")

Cry, my sweetheart, cry, cry, cry,
It's very sad when a friend has died,
It doesn't seem right, it doesn't seem fair,
The two of you made such a happy pair.

There's one thing that might help your grief:
Memories can bring such soothing relief.
Try to remember the happy days
When you were together, when you played.

Do you remember riding your bikes,
Going for walks, going for hikes?
(Friend's name) would want you to think of these;
Be happy you knew him *(her)* and he'll *(she'll)* be pleased.

Cry, my sweetheart, cry, cry, cry,
It's very sad when a friend has died.

RECIPES

Bake your child's favorite cookies to cheer him up, as the young boy's mom did in *The Tenth Good Thing about Barney*. Bake a favorite dessert of your late loved one and share it in her memory. Or bake something you like to give to others who share your grief.

LUSCIOUS LEMON BREAD
1. Preheat oven to 350 degrees.
2. Beat together ⅓ cup margarine and ¾ cup sugar until light and fluffy.
3. Add 2 eggs, one at a time, beating well after each one.
4. Sift together 1½ cups flour, 1½ teaspoons baking powder, and ¼ teaspoon salt; and add alternately with ½ cup milk.
5. Add ½ cup chopped walnuts and the grated rind of 1 lemon.
6. Turn batter into a greased 8-by-4-inch loaf pan. Bake for 50-60 minutes.
   Makes one loaf.

APRICOT NUT BREAD
1. Preheat oven to 350 degrees.
2. Mix together: 2½ cups flour, ½ cup sugar, 3½ teaspoons baking powder, ½ teaspoon salt, 1 tablespoon plus 1 teaspoon grated orange peel, 3 tablespoons oil, ½ cup milk, ¾ cup orange juice, 1 egg, 1 cup finely chopped walnuts, and 1 cup finely cut-up dried apricots. Beat well.
3. Pour into a 9-by-5-by-3-inch greased and floured loaf pan.
4. Bake for 55-65 minutes.

ACTIVITIES

MEMORY LIST

As suggested in **The Tenth Good Thing about Barney**, one constructive way to handle grief is to make a list of good things about the deceased. Reminiscing about the good times helps preserve all the happy memories. So sit down with your child and write down 10 good things about, or 10 happy times that she remembers spending with, her late loved one, and try to keep those memories alive.

MEMORY BOX

Take an empty shoebox and cover the lid with contact paper; or cover the lid with construction paper and then put on pressed dried flowers or other decoration that your child chooses—cover those things with clear contact paper to preserve and protect the top.

Inside the box you can put pictures or other memorabilia that your child might wish to collect.

PLANT A MEMORY PLANT

Help your child plant a living tree, a perennial flower or bulb, or a bush in honor of her loved one that will continue to grow and flourish in his name. If the weather is inappropriate, buy an indoor flower to grow inside until the weather warms up and the two of you can transplant it outdoors.

FOURTH WEEK

Pumpkin Time

Some of my fondest memories of Halloween are pumpkin-related: hayrides out into an orange-speckled field to handpick my very own pumpkin; designing and decorating my own funny-faced, toothless jack-o'-lantern; toasting pumpkin seeds for a crunchy tasty treat; and mashing up the pumpkin pulp to use it in various yummy desserts. Pumpkins add to the Halloween season in many forms. Plain, painted, or carved, they make attractive decorations on front steps, on front lawns, in windows, and on tables. And whether used for their seeds or for their pulp, they have a unique and flavorful taste and make delicious breads, muffins, cookies, and pies. With pumpkins in abundance and with a list of exciting things to do with them, now is your chance to spend a little pumpkin time with your little pumpkin.

READINGS

The Biggest Pumpkin Ever by Steven Kroll (Holiday House)

Two mice love and nurture the same growing pumpkin, neither knowing about the other one. The result is the biggest pumpkin ever. However, they want to use the pumpkin in different ways, and have to seek a compromise.

The Mystery of the Flying Orange Pumpkin by Steven Kellogg (Dial Books)

A neighborhood effort to grow a Halloween jack-o'-lantern comes to a halt when a crabby neighbor moves in. Not wanting to be deprived of the goal for which they worked so hard, the pumpkin-growers devise a clever plan, and all ends happily on Halloween Day.

Mousekin's Golden Pumpkin by Edna Miller (Prentice-Hall)

Through the eyes of a little mouse a pumpkin can be a glorious home.

RECITINGS

TEN LITTLE PUMPKINS
(Sung to "Ten Little Indians")

One little, two little, three little pumpkins,
Four little, five little, six little pumpkins,
Seven little, eight little, nine little pumpkins,
Ten little pumpkins round.

Three will be carved with great big smiles,
Three will have faces of monster styles,
Four will have teeth like a crocodile,
Ten pumpkins that I found.

HERE WE GO 'ROUND THE PUMPKIN PATCH
(Sung to "Here We Go 'Round the Mulberry Bush")

Here we go 'round the pumpkin patch,
The pumpkin patch, the pumpkin patch;
Here we go 'round the pumpkin patch
On a bright October morning. *(Walk around room as if looking for pumpkins in patch.)*

This is the way we choose our pumpkin,
Choose our pumpkin, choose our pumpkin;
This is the way we choose our pumpkin
On a bright October morning. *(Bend down as if picking.)*

Johnny wants the tiniest one,
The tiniest one, the tiniest one;
Johnny wants the tiniest one
To paint for Halloween morning. *(Hold hands in tiny ball.)*

Mary wants the biggest one,
The biggest one, the biggest one;
Mary wants the biggest one
To carve for Halloween morning. *(Hold hands in huge ball.)*

Peter wants the tastiest one,
The tastiest one, the tastiest one;
Peter wants the tastiest one
For pie on Halloween morning. *(Pretend to be eating pie.)*

RECIPES

There are so many pumpkin recipes; here are two of my favorites.

PUMPKIN SEEDS
1. Rinse seeds from your jack-o'-lantern.
2. Preheat oven to 350 degrees.
3. Melt 3 or 4 tablespoons of margarine and add a dash of Worcestershire sauce.
4. Mix together with the seeds.
5. Spread the seeds out on a cookie sheet and sprinkle them with a little salt, if desired.
6. Bake the seeds for about 10 minutes or until they are brown and crispy. Stir from time to time.

PERFECT PUMPKIN COOKIES
1. Preheat oven to 350 degrees.
2. Combine 2 cups flour, 1 cup uncooked quick oats, 1 teaspoon baking soda, 1 teaspoon cinnamon, and 1/2 teaspoon salt.
3. Cream 1 cup margarine, 1 cup firmly packed brown sugar, and 1/2 cup granulated sugar. Beat until fluffy.
4. Add 1 egg and 1 teaspoon vanilla; mix well.
5. Alternate additions of dry ingredients and 1 cup solid pack pumpkin, mixing well after each addition.
6. Stir in 1 cup chocolate bits or 1 cup raisins.
7. For each cookie, drop 1/4 cup dough onto lightly greased cookie sheet; spread into pumpkin shape using a thin metal spatula. Add a bit more dough to form a stem.

8. Bake 20 to 25 minutes, until the cookies are firm and lightly browned.

9. Remove from cookie sheets; cool on racks. Decorate with icings or peanut butter to affix raisins and/or nuts as eyes, noses, and mouths.

Makes about 20 cookies.

ACTIVITIES

SITTING PUMPKIN

Help your child with the following directions:

1. Trace and cut out 8 circles from orange construction paper, allowing the circles to be about 6 inches in diameter.

2. Fold each circle in half and apply a small amount of glue to one-half of the back side.

3. Attach this glued semi-circle to the back half of another folded circle.

4. Continue this process until all the folded circles are glued into an adjoining circle.

5. Make arms and legs out of black strips of construction paper by folding the paper back and forth in an accordion style and glue them to the body.

6. Make hands and feet and add them too.

7. Make facial features from scraps and attach them by folding back small tabs on which to put the glue.

8. Find a suitable place to seat your pumpkin.

PUMPKIN COLORING

1. Draw a large simple pumpkin (with stem) on white paper.

2. Sketch in two eyes, a nose, and a mouth.

3. Divide the pumpkin up into sections, first making the vertical curved lines that a pumpkin naturally has, then further dividing these spaces into smaller sections.

4. Number each section according to a color coding you choose—for example, #1 green, #2 orange, and #3 yellow. Then you would number the stem #1, the eyes, nose, and mouth #3, and the other sections #2. Give your child the paper, the appropriate crayons, and the directions, and let him color.

DECORATIVE DOUGHY PUMPKINS

1. Preheat oven to 350 degrees.

2. Combine 1 cup salt and 4 cups flour. Add enough water to make dough pliable (about 1 1/2 cups).

3. Knead for about 5 minutes, adding more flour if too sticky. Let your child do some kneading too!

4. Take a small ball of dough; shape it into a small pumpkin shape. Pat the dough flat, and put a hole in the top, using the tip of a knife.

5. Place the dough on a cookie sheet. Bake for 1 hour. Let cool.

6. Have your child paint and decorate jack-o'-lantern with tempera paint, then varnish.

7. Your child may wish to paste on black felt facial features, then put a piece of string through the hole and use the creation as a necklace or a window ornament.

FIFTH WEEK

Halloween—A Holiday of Delight and Fright

Soon it will be Halloween night, a holiday that is a bizarre combination of delight and fright. Part of the thrill of Halloween is the sheer pleasure of all of the trick-or-treating loot each child collects during her neighborhood jaunt. When else could she so quickly accumulate so much chocolate and sugar and be allowed to keep it . . . all in light of a holiday! The other part of Halloween's intrigue is the titillating subconscious desire to be frightened. Only in honor of this holiday do most of us indulge in wearing hideous monster masks, carving spooky evil-looking jack-o'-lanterns, and decorating our homes with the most morbid and eerie things we can find.

Halloween can be a nightmare for a little one (ages 2-3) who can't distinguish between reality and fantasy. A monster mask on a child is perceived as a real monster. Be cautious and conscious of your toddler's perception of this holiday, and if you sense any timidity, keep her busy in a room away from the trick-or-treating traffic to avoid any unnecessary fears and tears.

To add to the spooky atmosphere that naturally goes with the territory, here are some suggestions to augment your Halloween plans.

READINGS

Arthur's Halloween by Marc Brown (Little; pb Atlantic Monthly Press)

Arthur is feeling somewhat apprehensive and squeamish about Halloween to begin with, and when his little sister disappears into the witch's house while out trick-or-treating with him, he gets very nervous. Arthur's brotherly love helps him muster up enough courage to help his sister, and in the process he conquers his Halloween fears.

That Terrible Halloween Night by James Stevenson (Greenwillow Books)

Mary Ann and Louie are treated to another one of Grandpa's fabulous stories. This one relates a most terrifying tale of a Halloween night that Grandpa remembers from when he was young. James Stevenson's clever twist at the end of this story adds to this already exceptional Halloween book.

It's Halloween by Jack Prelutsky (Greenwillow Books)

This book contains thirteen spooky poems about Halloween, from "The Tricksters" to "Haunted House."

RECITINGS

THREE WHITE GHOSTS
(Sung to "Three Blind Mice")
Three white ghosts,
Three white ghosts—
See how they run,
See how they run.
They all came knocking on my front door,
Collecting candy and treats galore.
I gave them some but they wanted more,
Those three white ghosts.

GO 'ROUND AND 'ROUND THE NEIGHBORHOOD
(Sung to "Go 'Round and 'Round the Village")

Go 'round and 'round the neighborhood,
Go 'round and 'round the neighborhood,
Go 'round and 'round the neighborhood,
As we trick or treat tonight.

Collecting lots of candy,
Collecting lots of candy,
Collecting lots of candy,
As we trick or treat tonight.

We'll see so many costumes, *etc.*

Such fun on Halloween, *etc.*

MUSIC

The three sources listed below will provide good background music for Halloween project-making, Halloween eating, welcoming Halloween trick-or-treaters, or whenever you want to create "the mood."

■ *The Sorcerer's Apprentice*—by Dukas
■ *Danse Macabre*—by Saint-Saëns
■ *The Chilling, Thrilling Sounds of the Haunted House*—a Disneyland recording of sounds such as "Screams and Groans," "Thunder," "Lightning and Rain," and "A Collection of Creaks"

RECIPES

HALLOWEEN SUPPER
Eating dinner will probably not be a priority on Halloween night, so plan a quick and festive meal that will add to the excitement of the evening.

WITCHES' BREW
Mix the following ingredients together and simmer on the stove for 10 minutes: 2 cups apple juice or apple cider, 1/2 cup orange juice, 1/2 cup cranberry juice, 1/4 teaspoon cinnamon or 1 cinnamon stick, and 2 cloves.

PUMPKIN PIZZA
Begin with a pizza of your liking; it doesn't matter whether you make your own, buy one at the grocery store, or order one from a pizzeria. Nor does it matter if it is a cheese pizza or one with "the works."

Cut a green pepper into jack-o'-lantern eyes, nose, and mouth—any shapes you wish. Place them on the cooked pizza in the appropriate places.

Outline the pizza with black olives that have been halved.

Forget about dessert tonight for obvious reasons!

ACTIVITIES

HALLOWEEN DRAWINGS
Have your child make white chalk drawings on black paper to add to the other ghostly decorations in the house. He can draw witches, skeletons, ghosts, owls, bats, and/or spiders. Dipping the chalk in sugar water first will help keep it from smearing.

STRAW SKELETONS
Give your child a piece of black construction paper. Cut some white straws into various lengths and have her assemble them on the black construction paper to resemble the bones in a skeleton.

Glue the straws down one at a time.

The head in the form of a skull can be cut from white paper.

INDOOR DECORATIONS

Decorate the inside of your home for Halloween night with:

■ white sheets covering the furniture to give the house an unlived-in look;

■ yellow, green, blue, or red 25-watt bulbs in place of the normal white bulbs for some of your lamps to give a haunted house effect;

■ cut-out paper bats and spiders suspended from the ceiling;

■ any other store-bought decorations you wish to add, like skeletons or monsters.

OUTDOOR DECORATIONS

Decorate the outside of your home for Halloween night with:

■ scary-looking jack-o'-lanterns on the front steps or in the windows;

■ white-sheet ghosts hung from trees or over bushes;

■ stuffed scarecrow-like dummies sitting in lawn chairs. (Together with your child, select a pair of old pants and an old shirt and stuff them with newspaper. Tuck the shirt into the pants; lean them on the lawn chair. For the head, stuff a grocery bag with newspaper, tie it up, and decorate it with facial features. Stuff it into the shirt and put an old hat on top.)

CHAPTER ELEVEN

NOVEMBER
A Month of Preparation and Thanksgiving

November sends living things into a flurry of activity as they get ready for cold weather. People and animals alike head for warmer grounds, whether it is indoors by the wood-burning stove or outdoors in cozy underground burrows. The last of the crops are picked by people and animals alike, too. Human hands are busy canning applesauce and apple butter; animal paws are busy stockpiling for the long winter months. November is also the month in which Americans celebrate Thanksgiving. It affords us a rich opportunity to look at our past with pride and at our present with thankful hearts.

FIRST WEEK

An Apple a Day

America's love for apples is almost as old as America itself. Just a few years after the Pilgrims arrived in Massachusetts, the first apple seeds were planted. Since they were relatively easy to grow and the fruit was delicious and useful in cooking, apple trees began sprouting everywhere. Around this time a man by the name of John Chapman helped the apple's popularity explode. Johnny Appleseed, as he became affectionately known, loved apples and devoted his life to spreading them throughout America. He would gather apple seeds from cider presses, load his filled sacks on horseback, walk barefoot from settlement to settlement, and plant apple trees. Through his love, generosity, and care, Johnny Appleseed started America on its love affair with apples.

Today we have over three thousand varieties of apples, with an expanded recipe card file of ways to enjoy them. Before the local fresh apples are gone for another year, take some time with the "apple of your eye" and do some of the projects below.

READINGS

The Seasons of Arnold's Apple Tree by Gail Gibbons (Harcourt Brace Jovanovich)

Arnold has an apple tree that is his very own place to go. He enjoys watching the changes that occur to his tree each season and likes to find different things to do with his apple tree throughout the year. From springtime's apple blossom wreath to autumn's apple pie, Arnold finds apple tree treats. The reader will not only witness the gradual transformation of an apple tree, but will also be delighted with the various apple ideas Arnold invents.

Apple Pie by Anne Wellington (Prentice-Hall)

Mr. Bingle's apple tree is so productive it provides him with apples for his delicious pie for a long time. But on the day when there is only one apple left to pick, Mr. Bingle has a problem to solve. The apple is up too high for him to reach it. With his neighbors' helpful suggestions he finally succeeds and the story ends in a very topsy-turvy, happy way.

Apples, How They Grow by Bruce McMillan (Houghton Mifflin Co.)

Clear, close-up photography accompanied by simple text for younger children, as well as more in-depth text for more advanced readers, are used in this book to show the stages of development in a growing apple.

RECITINGS

HERE WE GO 'ROUND THE APPLE TREE
(Sung to "Here We Go 'Round the Mulberry Bush")

Here we go 'round the apple tree,
The apple tree, the apple tree—
Here we go 'round the apple tree
To pick some apples for you and me.

Make them into applesauce,
Applesauce, applesauce—
Make them into applesauce
Applesauce for you and me.

Cut them up for apple pie,
Apple pie, apple pie—
Cut them up for apple pie,
Apple pie for you and me.

Add other verses for other things you do with your apples.

SO MANY CHOICES

I picked a peck of apples,
So ripe and rosy red.
I think I'll make some applesauce—
No, apple crisp instead.

Perhaps I'll make some apple squares,
An apple pie, maybe.
Apple muffins are a treat
For the kids and me.

I've always loved apple turnovers
Or ice cream on apple cake.
It's so easy to go and pick them,
But so hard to choose what to bake!

RECIPES

In addition to apple pies and applesauce, for which you may already have your own favorite recipes, apples make other delicious treats. Try these two tasty ones.

STUFFED BAKED APPLES

1. Preheat oven to 350 degrees.
2. Make a hole through the center of two apples. You may use an apple corer or a knife. The hole should go through the entire apple.
3. Mix 1/2 cup granola, 2 tablespoons chopped nuts, 2 tablespoons wheat germ, and 2 tablespoons honey in a large mixing bowl. Fill each apple hole with the mixture. Top the apples with any extra filling.
4. Place each apple in a custard cup or other round cup that will fit the apple and pour 1/8 cup cider around each apple.
5. Cover each cup with aluminum foil and seal the edges by folding the foil tightly around the rim.
6. Bake for 45 minutes. The apples should be easily pierced with a fork when done.
7. Top each apple with 3 tablespoons vanilla yogurt, if desired. Serve warm.

APPLE CAKE PIE

1. Preheat oven to 350 degrees.
2. Melt ½ cup margarine over low heat. Remove from heat and blend with ¾ cup sugar and 1 egg, slightly beaten.
3. Add 1 cup flour, 1 teaspoon baking powder, 1 teaspoon cinnamon, ½ teaspoon salt, ½ teaspoon nutmeg, ⅛ teaspoon cloves, 1 teaspoon vanilla, 2 cups chopped apples, and ½ cup pecans. Mix well.
4. Pour into thoroughly greased 9-inch pie pan. Bake for 40-45 minutes.
5. Serve warm with ice cream. Serves 6.

ACTIVITIES

BOBBING FOR APPLES

This is an old-time favorite game to do whether at a party or at home with your own family. Simply fill a large tub halfway with water, put as many apples in as you need (one per person), and let each person attempt to grab an apple by using only his mouth! Depending on the ages of the participants, you may wish to supply such things as plastic tablecloths underneath the tub, headbands, or aprons.

APPLE IDENTIFICATION

The next time you are food shopping, whether at a grocery store or a farm, find as many different kinds of apples as you can. Try to identify them with your child by color, size, and taste, as mentioned below.

A few to look for are:

■ Macintosh—medium size, dark red with stripes, juicy and a bit tart

■ Golden Delicious—medium to large, yellow, sweet, firm and crisp

■ Red Delicious—medium to large, deep red color, five "knobs" on the blossom end, firm and sweet

■ Cortland—medium to large size, striped red, mildly tart

■ Winesap—small to medium size, bright red with scattered white dots, juicy, hard, crisp, and tart

■ Baldwin—large size, red, hard, juicy, tart.

See what others are available in your area.

APPLE SEED ARTWORK

Whenever apples are eaten, save the seeds to use at a later time. When you have an ample supply saved up, have your child try gluing them in various patterns, to make pictures, designs, and decorations.

APPLE STAR

Have you ever cut an apple open horizontally to see the star inside? Try it, and show it to your child. Let her eat one half and perhaps use the other half to make a great print by rubbing ink or paint over it, then pressing it onto white paper.

SECOND WEEK

Winter Is Coming

Temperatures are dropping, daylight hours are decreasing—winter must be coming. Now is the time to prepare for this chilly season. Everywhere you look, everyone seems to be doing his own thing in preparation. Animals are scurrying about gathering food to last them through the cold winter months. Homeowners are raking up the last of the leaves and preparing the yard for the first snowfall. Gardeners are canning or freezing the last of the garden vegetables. Children are putting away the sandbox and summer toys. Below are listed some activities for to do with your child to help you get ready before the snow flies.

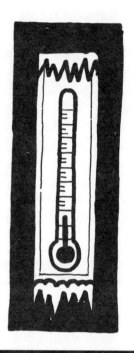

READINGS

Frederick by Leo Lionni (Pantheon; pb Knopf)

A busy family of field mice prepares for winter—four by gathering corn, nuts, wheat, and straw, and Frederick in his own unique way. Leo Lionni writes appealing animal stories with realistic characters—*Frederick* is no exception.

Has Winter Come? by Wendy Watson (William Collins & World Publishing Co.)

As the first snowflakes begin to fall, Mother and Father Woodchuck teach their children how to tell winter is in the air.

Winter's Coming by Eve Bunting (Harcourt Brace Jovanovich)

From Grandma to the hornets, everyone in this book is getting ready for the long cold winter that is approaching. Gently presented, the story gives many signs to look for as winter comes.

RECITINGS

HUSTLE BUSTLE
(Sung to "Ten Little Indians")

One little, two little, three squirrels a-hustle,
Four little, five little, six chipmunks bustle,
Seven little, eight little, nine mice a-rustle,
Gathering up seeds and nuts.

Nine little, eight little, seven mice a-burrow,
Six little, five little, four chipmunks furrow,
Three little, two little, one squirrel says, "Let's go,"
As the very first snowflake falls.

WINTER'S COMING SOON
(Sung to "Farmer in the Dell")

Winter's coming soon,
Winter's coming soon.
It is great and I can't wait—
Winter's coming soon.

Daddy rakes the leaves,
Daddy rakes the leaves.
Great big piles, I'll jump awhile—
Daddy rakes the leaves.

Mommy cans some food,
Mommy cans some food.
Beans and beets are such good treats—
Mommy cans some food.

The animals gather nuts,
The animals gather nuts.
They know, too, to gather food, so
The animals gather nuts.

Yes, winter's coming soon,
Winter's coming soon.
It is great and I can't wait—
Winter's coming soon.

RECIPES

WINTER ENERGY SNACK

1. Preheat oven to 350 degrees.
2. Heat 6 tablespoons of honey and 1/4 cup margarine in a pan until blended.
3. Pour over 6 cups of popped popcorn and 1 cup unsalted peanuts, stirring as you pour.
4. When the popcorn and nuts are well-coated, spread it on a pan in a single layer. Bake for 5-10 minutes or until crisp, stirring several times.
5. After the mix cools, add some or all of the following: raisins, carob chips, sesame sticks, and cashews or any other nut you may like.
6. Divide up into small plastic bags. Put twist ties or colorful ribbons around each bag, and enjoy a portion one day when you need a winter energy boost.

THUMBPRINT NUTTY COOKIES

1. Preheat oven to 350 degrees.
2. Mix thoroughly 1/4 cup softened butter, 1/4 cup margarine, 1/4 cup packed brown sugar, 1 egg yolk, and 1/2 teaspoon vanilla. Work in 1 cup flour and 1/4 teaspoon salt until dough holds together. Shape dough by teaspoonfuls into 1-inch balls.
3. Beat 1 egg white slightly. Dip each dough ball into egg white; then roll in 3/4 cup finely chopped walnuts.

4. Place 1 inch apart on ungreased cookie sheet; press thumb deeply in center of each.
5. Bake about 10 minutes or until light brown.
6. Immediately remove from cookie sheet. Cool. Fill thumbprint with jellies or nuts.
   Makes about 3 dozen cookies.

PRE-WINTER COLLECTIONS

In preparation for some very cold winter days when indoor play will be the only play possible, here are two collections you can begin now to save for later uses.

1. Collect indoor materials to have on hand for future collages and art projects—for example, yarn, material, construction paper, ribbon, small containers of interesting and varying sizes and shapes, bottle caps, plastic forks and spoons, straws. Put them all in a large bag, box, or basket and keep adding to the collection.
2. Collect dried materials for future artwork as you and your child take a nature walk outdoors. Look for weeds, twigs, flowers, grasses, pods, pine cones, and/or twigs.

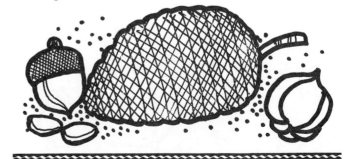

ACTIVITIES

FREEFORM FALL ARRANGEMENTS

This is a nice reminder of the sunny outdoors for those long, cold, wintry days.

Give your child a margarine tub or other small container. Have him put clay, play dough, or other substitute material inside holder. Insert dried materials from above-mentioned nature walk to make an original dried flower arrangement.

INSIDE TREE

Fill a small flowerpot with soil. Find a well-shaped branch, or several smaller branches. Push it far enough into the potted soil to hold it upright. Keep the soil moist and the branches will continue to remain fresh and green for quite a while. Have your child draw birds and color them on both sides so that they are vivid and alive-looking. Tie or staple them to the branches in natural positions. This is another great reminder of the outdoors when you have to stay in; you can keep it and decorate it according to the various holidays.

STYROFOAM ART

Give your child a piece of Styrofoam, any shape that she wishes, and arrange dried materials by sticking the materials into the Styrofoam.

THIRD WEEK

A Time for Giving Thanks

Did you know that the first Thanksgiving feast lasted for three days? Considering that the Pilgrims would have perished without the tremendous help from their Indian friends, three days was conservative! In addition to a whopping feast that included wild turkey, squash, corn, Indian pudding, fruits, and nuts, there was entertainment in the form of military drills performed by the Pilgrims and Indian dancing and singing.

Our Thanksgiving feasts today are reminiscent of that first one with traditional foods like turkey and "squash" pie, and with the holiday's purpose: to give thanks. As you prepare for your Thanksgiving this year, consider some of the suggestions below. They may add some personal meaning to the holiday for you and your family.

READINGS

Thanksgiving Day by Gail Gibbons (Holiday House)

Using simple, colorful illustrations and straightforward, clear text, Gail Gibbons tells the story of Thanksgiving—its origins, traditions, and celebrations.

Cranberry Thanksgiving by Wende and Harry Devlin (Parent's Magazine Press)

Every year for Thanksgiving Maggie and her grandmother invite a guest to share in their Thanksgiving feast. This year Grandmother has invited Mr. Horace, a kind, crisply-dressed gentleman who lives alone; and Maggie invites Mr. Whiskers, a clam-digging, whiskery old sea captain who hasn't had a Thanksgiving dinner in twenty years. Grandmother has always mistrusted Mr. Whiskers, but when someone steals her famous recipe for cranberry bread (for which bakers all over the countryside have offered a lot of money) an unexpected ending unfolds. This book is the first of a series of cranberry mysteries that involve Maggie and her grandmother. An extra bonus is the inclusion of the famous cranberry bread recipe.

Molly's Pilgrim by Barbara Cohen (Lothrop, Lee & Shepard)

Molly is a little Russian girl who comes to America with her family to escape the Cossacks. She is unhappy because the other children in school make fun of her. But one day she changes their minds.

RECITINGS

THE PILGRIMS AND THE INDIANS
(Sung to "Ten Little Indians")
In 1620 some people decided
To leave their country where they resided.
They boarded the *Mayflower* all united,
To sail to a better land.

Ten brave, twenty brave, thirty brave Pilgrims,
Forty brave, fifty brave, sixty brave Pilgrims,
Seventy brave, eighty brave, ninety, and
  twelve more,
Came to America.

The first year was tough, the weather was bitter.
Forty-seven Pilgrims died that winter.
Food was scarce and life was grimmer
For those that remained.

But then came the Indians, friendly and kind.
They showed the Pilgrims food to find.
They taught them tricks on how to survive—
Thanks to the Indians.

A feast was planned to show their gratitude.
The Pilgrims prepared their harvested food.
Governor Bradford invited the Indians
To celebrate with them.

Ten kind, twenty kind, thirty kind Indians,
Forty kind, fifty kind, sixty kind Indians,
Seventy kind, eighty kind, ninety kind Indians
Joined the Thanksgiving feast.

The Pilgrims and Indians feasted for three days,
They danced, sang songs, and shared games
    to play,
The Pilgrims and Indians had found a great way
To live as friends in peace.

THANKS, THANKS
(Sung to "Rain, Rain")

Thanks, thanks,
Give thanks today,
On this great Thanksgiving day,
Relatives will come to stay,
We just love this holiday.

Thanks, thanks
For many things—
Love and care that family brings,
Friends to play with and to sing,
Thanks, thanks for everything.

RECIPES

CRANBERRY BREAD

1. Preheat oven to 350 degrees.
2. Sift 2 cups white flour, 2 cups whole wheat flour, 1/2 cup brown sugar, 1/2 cup white sugar, 1/2 teaspoon cinnamon, 1/4 teaspoon nutmeg, 1 tablespoon baking powder, 1/2 teaspoon salt, and 1 teaspoon baking soda into a large bowl.
3. Cut in 1/2 cup margarine until mixture is crumbly.
4. Add 2 beaten eggs, 1 tablespoon grated orange peel, and 1 1/2 cups orange juice all at once; stir just until mixture is evenly moist.
5. Fold in 1 1/2 cups light raisins, 2 cups chopped cranberries, and 1 1/2 cups chopped nuts.
6. Spoon into 2 greased and floured 9-by-5-by-3-inch loaf pans. Bake for 1 hour, or until a toothpick inserted in the center comes out clean. Remove from pan; cool on a wire rack.

You may substitute cranberries for the raisins to have an all-cranberry bread.

RUBY APPLESAUCE

Delicious served with turkey, chicken, or pork, or over potato pancakes.

1. Wash 1 16-ounce package cranberries and place in 3-quart saucepan.
2. Add 1 1/2 cups sugar and 2 tart apples, diced.
3. Place pan, covered, over medium heat; when cover is hot, reduce heat to low and simmer about 10 minutes.
4. Stir in 1/2 teaspoon ground cinnamon, 1/4 teaspoon nutmeg, and 1/8 teaspoon ground cloves.

Serve hot or cold.

ACTIVITIES

I AM THANKFUL FOR . . .

Help your child to make a list of 10 things for which she is thankful. Write them on something as plain as a piece of paper, or make an Indian headdress out of construction paper and write the 10 things on the headdress feathers. You can also make a simple turkey and write the 10 things on the paper turkey feathers. (One simple turkey to make could be as follows: Draw a large shape that looks like an unshelled peanut standing on end. Draw two eyes on it, color it, and add two stick figure legs on the bottom. Then take colored pieces of construction paper and cut out 10 feathers to stick behind this turkey body.)

THANKSGIVING CARDS

These homemade cards can either be mailed to friends or relatives or given to each person who is sharing your Thanksgiving feast with you.

1. Spread finger paint on paper.
2. Press your child's hand (palm side down) in the paint, cover it well, and then make a good imprint by pushing the painted hand down on a piece of construction paper that has been cut and folded into an appropriate card.
3. When the handprint has dried, add stick figure legs at the base of the hand and one eye and wattle on the thumb section. Then write, "Dear _____, Thank you for _____," either on the top or bottom of the turkey or inside the card if you are folding it.

CLOTHESPIN PUPPETS

In *Molly's Pilgrim*, the children in Molly's class make clothespin puppets of Indians or Pilgrims. You can make some, too. Use the knob of the clothespin as the head and with a felt marker draw in facial features. Then dress the figure with appropriate Indian or Pilgrim clothes (drawn on paper and cut out, or cut from material). Use the puppets as decorations or put together a little skit to entertain the guests at your Thanksgiving feast.

FEATHER GAME

Cut out feathers of different colors and put them in a large bag. Have your child pull one feather out and name something he is thankful for that is the color of that feather.

FOURTH WEEK

Thanksgiving Empathy

As babies and toddlers our children have very egocentric views of the world. Everything and everyone exists for them. There is nothing negative about this self-centeredness—it is merely a baby's lack of being able to comprehend the existence of others. It isn't until around the age of three that a child first begins to show a glimmer of empathy towards others, as you can observe when they play with their peers. A gradual reaching out and sharing begins to develop.

Since we, as parents, would like our children to be empathetic and compassionate, we must do our best to encourage their social growth. Helping them to appreciate how others feel is extremely important. Being able to see both sides of a situation is invaluable. Thanksgiving presents a good situation to study two sides of a picture. How did the Pilgrims feel leaving their homes to travel to a new, unfamiliar land? How did the Indians feel having to share their land with these strangers? Try to pose similar scenes for your child and help her appreciate the feelings of both parties involved.

This chapter's activities center around the turkey, a traditional Thanksgiving symbol. Practice your empathy in a comical way and try to imagine how turkeys feel around this time of year!

READINGS

One Tough Turkey: A Thanksgiving Story by Steven Kroll (Holiday)

Did the Pilgrims really have turkey at their first Thanksgiving dinner? According to this book, Solomon, one tough turkey, made sure they didn't! When he saw the Pilgrims coming after him he planned a counterattack that surprised all. This humorous account of the first Thanksgiving is very entertaining.

Little Bear's Thanksgiving by Janice Brustlein (Lothrop, Lee & Shepard Co.)

When Little Bear's friend, Goldie, invites him to Thanksgiving dinner he fears he won't be able to go, because Thanksgiving doesn't begin until he is deep into his winter sleep. With the help of all his animal friends Little Bear gets to enjoy his first Thanksgiving ever: but so do his friends.

Arthur's Thanksgiving by Marc Brown (Little, Brown & Co.)

When Arthur is chosen to be the director of the class Thanksgiving play, he is in for a tougher job than he expected. Trying to find someone to play the part of the turkey is almost impossible. But after several frustrating attempts Arthur comes up with the perfect solution.

RECITINGS

TURKEY TALK
(Sung to "On Top of Old Smokey")

I used to feel sad,
I was so depressed,
My life was a shambles,
My life was a mess.

I had a big problem,
I couldn't gain weight,
I was scrawny and puny
Regardless what I ate.

All my friends teased me,
They called me mean names,
They said I was worthless
And brought them all shame.

But then something happened
On the first of November,
That changed all my thinking,
I'll always remember.

Thanksgiving was coming.
Fat turkeys were sought.
I may be real puny,
But a dinner I'm not!

I'M A LITTLE TURKEY
(Sung to "I'm a Little Teapot")

I'm a little turkey, plump and round,
I keep in shape and I weigh thirty pounds.
When November comes I'll run around,
And hope that I will not be found.

RECIPES

TURKEY FRUIT CUP

These make tasty and festive appetizers.
1. Cut an orange in half, scoop out the center, and dice the fruit.
2. Add to the orange $1/2$ diced apple, $1/2$ diced banana, grapes cut in half and seeded, $1/2$ diced pear, and any other fruit you'd like to include in a fruit salad. Raisins, chopped nuts, and coconut are fun to add, too.
3. Fill the orange shells with the salad.
4. Add a toothpick for a neck, a carrot round for a head, and half a toothpick for a beak. Stick a few celery leaves in the back of the cup for feathers.

TURKEY SOUP

A great way to use Thanksgiving leftovers!
1. Fill a large pot $2/3$ full with water or with 3 cans of chicken broth. Bring to a boil.
2. Add turkey bones (with some meat left on them). Simmer 1 hour. Remove carcass and loose bones. Leave broth in pot.
3. Add $1/2$ cup diced carrot, $1/2$ cup cooked rice, barley or alphabet noodles, 2 diced potatoes, 1 chopped onion, 2 or 3 diced celery stalks, $1/2$ cup leftover stuffing, $1/2$ to 1 cup leftover gravy, minced parsley to taste, and salt and pepper to taste. Simmer for 30 minutes.

ACTIVITIES

TURKEYS GALORE

Turkeys can be made out of soap, potatoes, rocks, paper-bags, Styrofoam shapes, paper cups, cardboard tubes, paper plates, or any other materials you and your child choose. Use the basic object as the base of the turkey. Make feathers and wings out of colored construction paper or colored toothpicks. Attach a round head shape with a toothpick for the neck, and use toothpicks for the legs.

Turkey Mobile

Bend a wire coat hanger into a circular shape. Cover it with nylon stocking. Cut beak, wattle, feet, and feathers from construction paper and have your child glue these on. Use wiggly buttons for eyes. (Eyes, beak, and wattle in the center of the circle; the feet along the bottom edge of the coat hanger; and the feathers all along the outside rim of the hanger.) Use yarn to hang the turkeys wherever you'd like.

Giant Turkey Puppet

1. Begin with a large cardboard box as the body. Cut a hole in the bottom of the box. Turn it upside down and fit it over your child's body, with his head sticking out the cut-out hole.
2. Have the child wear red stockings for the turkey's legs.
3. Use a brown paper bag for the turkey's head. Cut out two large holes for eyes. Use a funnel for the turkey's nose and glue it where the nose should be. Cut a wattle out of red material and glue that on. Fit the bag over the child's head, making sure to line up the eye holes so that he can see well.

And there you have a walking, talking giant turkey puppet!

CHAPTER TWELVE

DECEMBER
A Festive Month

December is probably one of your child's favorite months, because of the excitement generated by the December holidays. By the time December rolls around children are anxiously preparing their wish lists for holiday gifts.

Some five- and six-year-olds might have a special request on their lists this year—"All I want for Christmas is my two front teeth"—for this is the age of wiggly teeth and jack-o'-lantern smiles.

Try not to overextend yourself during this very busy month. You want to have enough energy left over to welcome in the new year with your child, too! In this chapter you will find ideas for the holidays of Christmas, Hanukkah, and New Year's Eve as well as a few suggestions for those of you dealing with those first loose teeth.

FIRST WEEK

Get Ready for Those Loose Teeth

Do you remember those sleepless nights your uncomfortable teething infant and you endured? Can you think back to some of the crazy remedies you tried or said you'd try to help ease those swollen gums?

There is something that will erase all those unpleasant memories in a split second. You will know what it is as soon as you hear your child exclaim, "I have a loose tooth!" Then prepare yourself for the ensuing display of excitement you will witness. Losing one's first tooth means more than a change in one's appearance. It signifies a leap into "big kidhood." You, as a parent, may not be particularly ready to face the fact that your little one is growing up; but you handled her first steps, her first words, and her first day of school, so inevitably, you will get through this, too.

If your child was an early teether, most likely she will begin to lose her teeth early as well. Generally this major event takes place somewhere between the ages of five and seven. The books and projects in this chapter are good preparatory activities as well as fun things that your child can relate to when her teeth are actually wiggling around. Take some time now to discuss the importance of good dental hygiene, and then have some fun preparing for the day when your child says goodbye to baby tooth #1 and hello to a new stage in life.

READINGS

One Morning in Maine by Robert McCloskey (Viking; pb Penguin)

When Sal feels a loose tooth in her mouth for the first time, she knows her life will be different. This means she is a big girl now, and as the day progresses and her tooth falls out, her excitement grows.

Little Rabbit's Loose Tooth by Lucy Bate (Crown Publishers)

When Little Rabbit's loose tooth comes out in her chocolate ice cream, she isn't sure what she should do with it. Should she make something out of it or leave it for the tooth fairy? Her creative ideas are as enjoyable as the perfect ending.

Loose Tooth by Steven Kroll (Holiday House)

When Flapper's twin brother, Fang, loses a tooth first, Flapper is so jealous he resorts to drastic measures. But once he steals the tooth before the tooth fairy comes, he doesn't know what to do with it. This is a funny yet sensitive story about dealing with difficult emotions.

RECITINGS

BRUSH, BRUSH, BRUSH YOUR TEETH
(Sung to "Row, Row, Row Your Boat")
Brush, brush, brush your teeth,
As carefully as you can,
Ten on top, ten underneath,
That's our little plan.

(Change the number according to your child's particular number of teeth.)

MAKING CHANGES
(Sung to "Pop! Goes the Weasel")

All throughout the childhood years
A mouth is making changes.
A baby chews on all that's in sight, then,
Pop! There's a new tooth.

This goes on for two or three years,
Until a set of twenty is there,
Then at five or six—look out,
Pop! They fall out!

RECIPES

Sometimes those wiggly loose teeth need pampering with soft, easy-to-chew foods, and sometimes all they need is one bite into a crunchy, hard snack!

"TOOTH" RICE PUDDING
1. Cook 1 cup of uncooked brown rice in 1³/₄ cups of water. Bring to a boil, then reduce heat to simmer, cover the pan, and cook for approximately 45 minutes.
2. Combine the cooked rice with 1¹/₃ cups milk, ¹/₄ cup brown sugar, 1 tablespoon margarine, and 1 teaspoon vanilla. Stir in 1 teaspoon cinnamon and ¹/₂ cup raisins.
3. Put in a greased baking dish. Bake for about 50 minutes or until set. Serve warm in a cup or bowl with milk poured over the top.

"TOOTH-BREAKING" HARDTACK
This flatbread makes a crunchy good treat and is great with soup on a cold day.
1. Preheat oven to 425 degrees.
2. Mix ¹/₈ teaspoon baking soda and 3 tablespoons buttermilk.
3. In another bowl mix 1 cup flour, 4 teaspoons maple syrup, and ¹/₄ teaspoon salt.
4. Cut in 1¹/₂ tablespoons margarine to flour mixture.
5. Add buttermilk mixture.
6. Roll very thin. Put on a cookie sheet and cut into rectangles. Prick with a fork.
7. Bake until golden, about 5-10 minutes.

ACTIVITIES

Mom and/or Dad are the prime caretakers of a child's teeth for the first few years of life. But around age five, a child can begin to take an active role in his own dental hygiene. To help your child learn and want to participate in this important daily deed, make a game about brushing teeth, make up a fun song while you brush, or practice on each other or on dolls or puppets.

MOTHER, MAY I
Adapt this familiar game to make it a teeth-brushing activity. Divide the mouth up into four sections: top right, top left, bottom right, and bottom left. Take turns giving commands such as, "You may brush your top right teeth straight up and down five times." Remember the key to this game is that before the player can do what the command is, he must first say, "Mother, may I?" The reward at the end can be a big tall glass of

water or whatever is appropriate for your family. If the players forget to say, "Mother, may I?" they have to start all over and re-brush those sections that they have already brushed.

FUNNY TEETH

Just how important are our teeth to our appearance? What does it look like to be toothless or to have unattractive teeth? Take an old magazine that is destined for the garbage and allow your child to erase the teeth on the pictures and perhaps fill in some crooked, funny-looking teeth. See how it changes one's looks!

TOOTH POUCH

This is a great pouch for your child to put his fallen-out tooth in before he slips it under his pillow.

Very simply, cut a rectangle in a piece of material, fold it in half and sew up two sides, leaving the opening unsewn. Close the top by sewing a Velcro patch, a snap, a button, or a pull string through a folded-down edging. Decorate the pouch with cut-out felt teeth. Copy this poem to put in the pouch:

Dear Tooth Fairy,
In this pouch you will see
A tiny little tooth from me.
I'd like to trade my tooth with you—
Money, toys, or treats will do.

SECOND WEEK

It's Beginning to Look a Lot Like Christmas

Everywhere you look you can see colorful reminders that Christmas is just a few weeks away. Splashes of color speckle evergreen trees both inside and outside the home. Festive wreaths of reds and greens adorn fireplaces and windows. Sparkling light-catching garlands softly drape over doorways. Tiny twinkling white lights brighten branches and lampposts.

Yes, it is really beginning to look a lot like Christmas. *And* it is also beginning to smell, taste, feel, and sound a lot like Christmas. Use all five senses to explore this magical season with your child.

READINGS

Peter Spier's Christmas! by Peter Spier (Doubleday & Co.)

This wordless picture book depicts every Christmas scene imaginable, from the excitement of preholiday preparations to the inevitable family clean-up day, in Peter Spier's award-winning style. This is a truly wonderful book in which one's sense of sight is treated to holiday celebrations on every page.

The Sweet Smell of Christmas by Patricia Scarry (Western Publishing Co.)

In this Golden Scratch & Sniff book, Little Bear wakes up on Christmas Eve morning and knows something extraordinary is going to happen. "My nose tells me so." And he proceeds to experience six wonderful fragrances that he associates with Christmas. This is a treat for one's sense of smell.

Before reading this delightful book, gather the following items for your child to smell as an introductory activity: a piece of apple, a few pine needles, a candy cane, ginger (or a gingerbread cookie), chocolate, and a piece of an orange.

After reading add some of your own fragrances to extend the activity further.

A Sesame Street Christmas by Pat Tornborg (Western Publishing Co.)

This festive collection presents Christmas stories and poems, told by various Sesame Street characters, and directions for holiday snacks, toys, gifts, and ornaments.

RECITINGS

WE WISH YOU A MERRY CHRISTMAS
(Chorus)
We wish you a merry Christmas,
We wish you a merry Christmas,
We wish you a merry Christmas
And a happy New Year.

Let's all bake some Christmas cookies,
Let's all bake some Christmas cookies,
Let's all bake some Christmas cookies
And spread Christmas cheer.

Let's all wrap some Christmas presents, *(etc.)*

Let's all decorate our houses, *(etc.)*

(Pantomime each of the actions. Add more to your liking.)

CHRISTMAS IS COMING
(Sung to "Three Blind Mice")

Christmas is coming, Christmas is coming,
I'm so excited, I'm so excited.
I love the colorful Christmas lights
That decorate houses and trees at night.
I love the lovely sights that come when
Christmas is coming.

Christmas is coming, Christmas is coming,
I'm so excited, I'm so excited.
I love the baking of Christmas treats,
The cookies, cakes, and other sweets—
I love the smells and tastes that come when
Christmas is coming.

Christmas is coming, Christmas is coming,
I'm so excited, I'm so excited.
I love the musical sounds I hear
Christmas carolers are getting near.
I love the Christmas songs that come when
Christmas is coming.

Christmas is coming, Christmas is coming,
I'm so excited, I'm so excited.
I love the feeling that people have
Of being kind, giving, and glad.
I love the feeling that comes along when
Christmas is coming.

RECIPES

Since the senses of SMELL and TASTE are so closely related, you can doubly enjoy these Christmas treats.

CHRISTMAS GINGERBREAD FORMS
1. Preheat oven to 375 degrees.
2. Mix together 1 cup margarine, 3/4 cup honey, 1 egg, and 3/4 cup molasses.
3. Sift together 1 1/2 teaspoons baking soda, 1/4 teaspoon salt, 2 teaspoons ginger, 1 teaspoon cinnamon, 1 teaspoon cloves, and 5 cups flour.
4. Mix wet and dry ingredients.
5. Refrigerate dough until cold—about 2 hours—for easier handling.
6. Roll 1/4 inch thick on floured surface.
7. Cut with Christmas cookie cutters. Decorate with assorted raisins and nuts.
8. Bake for 10 minutes.

CHRISTMAS EGGNOG
1. Beat 1 egg.
2. Add 1 cup milk, 1 tablespoon sugar, and 1/2 teaspoon vanilla. Beat well with an eggbeater.
3. Sprinkle nutmeg on the top.

ACTIVITIES

A TOUCHING CHRISTMAS GAME

Collect various items that might represent the holiday season—for example, a bough of an evergreen tree, tinsel, candy cane, ornament, small wrapped gift, bow, ribbon, or cotton. Put all of the items in a grocery bag. Play a guessing game. Cover your child's eyes and let her reach into the bag and feel one item. Then have her try to guess what it is just from feeling it. Repeat the activity with the other objects. Let her gather a few items for you to try to guess, too.

GUESS THE PRESENT GAME

Collect several items of varying size and weight, enough boxes to wrap the items up, and some wrapping paper. Wrap each item and then let your child shake the box to try to determine what might be inside. To make it easier, let her see the various things you are going to wrap beforehand, and then she will only have to decide which one is in each box. Or, give her the added sense of touch and allow her to open the box and feel what is inside to help her determine the contents.

A CHRISTMAS HEARING GAME

There are countless Christmas albums to listen to—everyone from the Muppets to Bruce Springsteen has recorded his own special holiday tune. Enjoy whichever is your child's favorite, and when singing along, add some jingle bells, drums (makeshift—Tupperware and wooden spoons), or any other instrumentation you and your child wish.

Share your singing fun with others and go caroling—either around your own neighborhood, at a convalescent home, or just at a few friends' homes. Ask others to join you and enjoy your homemade music and each other's company.

Make a listening game out of the Christmas music that is so plentiful at this time of year. Get several Christmas albums from your local library. Play one song from one of the albums and have your child try to guess who is singing the particular song, and what the song is. See how quickly your child can guess—three notes into the song, six notes into the song?

THIRD WEEK

Hanukkah Happiness

Playing the dreidel game, giving gifts, and lighting candles for eight consecutive days are some of the traditional festivities Jews enjoy during the holiday of Hanukkah. Although Hanukkah, or the Festival of Lights, is not one of the major Jewish holidays, it is celebrated in December by most Jewish families. It is a time of joy and thanks as we remember a time when people were freed from religious oppression. Like every holiday, Hanukkah is celebrated differently according to each family's own unique flavors and traditions. (It is even spelled three different ways: Chanukah, Hanukah, and Hanukkah!)

Whether you celebrate Hanukkah with your family, have friends who do, or just want to learn more about this joyous holiday, the activities below will help.

READINGS

Potato Pancakes All Around—A Hanukkah Tale
by Marilyn Hirsh (Bonim Books)

Grandma Yetta and Grandma Sophie may not be able to agree on whose recipe for potato pancakes is best. But when Samuel, the peddler, insists that the best is from a crust of bread they do agree he is crazy. Samuel manages to prove to the whole family that his wonderful method is best in this humorous and very clever tale. The last two pages offer Grandma Yetta's and Grandma Sophie's recipe for potato pancakes and a brief explanation of the holiday of Hanukkah.

I Love Hanukkah by Marilyn Hirsh (Holiday House)

A little boy's grandfather tells him the story of this sacred Jewish celebration.

The Story of Chanukah for Children by Beverly Rae Charette (Ideals Publishing Corp.)

The history behind the holiday of Chanukah is told in easy flowing rhymes in this clearly told, pleasantly illustrated book.

RECITINGS

HANUKKAH

Let's shine up the menorah,
Put all eight candles up.
We'll light one every evening
As we sit down to sup.

Let's make some special food—
Grandma's latkes are the best.
Serve them warm and golden brown
With applesauce and the rest.

Let's play our favorite dreidel game,
We'll each take turns and spin.
Nun means you get nothing,
Gimmel means I win.

These are the ways we'll celebrate
Hanukkah this year.
With friends and all our relatives
Who are so very dear.

I'M A LITTLE DREIDEL
(Sung to "I'm a Little Teapot")

I'm a little dreidel
Made of clay,
Pick me up and a game we can play.
When I get a good spin,
Hear me say,
"Let's have some fun on this holiday!"

RECIPES

POTATO PANCAKES

1. Peel and grate 4 potatoes and one small onion. Pour off the extra liquid.
2. Add 2 eggs, 2 tablespoons bread crumbs, 1/2 teaspoon salt, and 1/2 teaspoon pepper. Mix very well.
3. Heat 1/2 cup oil in a frying pan on medium heat until it sizzles.
4. Carefully drop the batter by tablespoons into the hot oil. Flatten each pancake with a spatula.
5. When the pancakes are golden brown, carefully turn them over with the spatula. Fry the other side until brown and crisp.
7. Drain them on a paper towel while you make more.
  This will serve six people. Serve with applesauce.

DREIDEL COOKIES

A dreidel is a square-sided top which is used in a popular Hanukkah game. Make your favorite recipe for sugar cut-out cookies, then use a dreidel cookie cutter or draw a dreidel on cardboard, cut it out, then use it as a pattern to cut around the dough. Decorate the cookies with frosting.

ACTIVITIES

HOMEMADE MENORAH

You can make your own menorah out of many different media—an upside-down egg carton, upside-down paper cups, or birthday candle holders stuck into Styrofoam. Below you will find directions for making a braided clay menorah.

1. Take a lump of clay, any color, and divide it into three equal chunks.
2. Help your child roll each chunk into a long rope.
3. Braid the three ropes together. Wind them around to make a circle.
4. Flatten it out slightly so that it will stand well.
5. Your child can push eight birthday candles into the braid, equidistant from each other. Take one more small lump of clay to hold the ninth candle, the **shamash,** and attach it to the braid.

HANUKKAH MEMORY GAME

1. Place ten items on a tray. Items might include a dreidel, a Hanukkah candle, a menorah, a book about Hanukkah, a dime, a piece of candy, a penny, a raisin, or any other Hanukkah-related item.
2. Show them to the other players for an amount of time that you have previously determined.
3. Once the players have studied the tray filled with the items, take the tray away.
4. Either ask them to name as many of the items as they can remember, or remove one item and then have them look at the tray again to see if they can figure out what is missing.
5. The number of items you place on the tray and the amount of time you allow for them to study the tray should be determined by you according to the age and skills of the children playing.

HANUKKAH MAZES

Draw on paper some simple mazes that have Hanukkah themes. One might have the Maccabees trying to find their way to Jerusalem; another might have the Maccabees trying to find their way to a cruse of oil in the Temple. Do as many as you have time for.

FOURTH WEEK

'Tis the Night before Christmas

Christmas will soon be here, and no doubt your child's anticipation is at its peak! Are you ready for Santa's arrival? Are the stockings all hung by the chimney with care? Do you have Rudolph's carrots and Santa's snack all prepared?

This chapter has some fun-filled suggestions of activities for you and your child to do *for* Santa before he arrives.

READINGS

The Night Before Christmas by Clement Clarke Moore, illustrated by Tasha Tudor (Rand McNally & Co.)

There are many versions of this age-old popular poem by Clement Clarke Moore. Tasha Tudor's is one of the very beautiful ones. (Some others that are available include James Marshall's and Tomie de Paola's). No doubt this book is one that your child will eventually be reciting to you! Note the descriptive passages about Santa's looks and draw a picture including all of the details with your child.

Mousekin's Christmas Eve by Edna Miller (Prentice-Hall, Inc.)

Mousekin, a little white-footed mouse, sets out to find the comfort of a new home because his old home has been left cold and empty. What he finds is made twice as beautiful, for it is Christmas Eve and the peace and warmth of the season welcome him, too.

Merry Christmas, Strega Nonna by Tomie de Paola (Harcourt Brace Jovanovich)

Christmas has a magic of its own, and thus Strega Nonna, the village witch, will not use her magic to help with all the preparations needed to be done for her traditional Christmas Eve feast that she prepares for the whole town of Calabria. Big Anthony, usually known for his bumbling mistakes and incessant curiosity, proves he, too, can do some pretty magical things in this tender Christmas story.

RECITINGS

I LOVE CHRISTMAS

I love the excitement
As Christmas gets near.
I love Christmas carols
Sung this time of year.

I love playful guessing
As packages appear
Under our tree,
So full of good cheer.

I love the feel of Christmas,
Seeing friends so dear;
All problems and sadness
Seem to disappear.

Yes, I love Christmas so much,
This holiday so great,
Except for one tiny thing—
The WAIT!

IT'LL BE COMING BEFORE YOU KNOW IT
(Sung to "She'll Be Coming 'Round the Mountain")

It'll be coming before you know it,
Christmas Day—Hurray!
It'll be coming before you know it,
Christmas Day—Hurray!
It'll be coming before you know it,
It'll be coming before you know it,
It'll be coming before you know it,
Christmas Day—Hurray!

We'll be gathering together when it comes—Hello!
(etc.)

We'll exchange our gifts of love when it comes—
for you! *(etc.)*

We'll be sharing peace and joy when it comes—
love all! *(etc.)*

RECIPES

SANTA'S SUGAR COOKIES

These seem to be the most appropriate snack to leave for Santa, for as my sons said, "Santa has to have Santa cookies!"

1. Cream 1 cup softened margarine and 1 cup sugar together. Add 1 egg and mix well.
2. Combine 4 cups flour, 1 teaspoon baking powder, 1/2 teaspoon baking soda, 1/2 teaspoon salt, and 1/2 teaspoon nutmeg.
3. Alternately add dry ingredients with 1/2 cup sour cream and 1 teaspoon vanilla to creamed mixture.
4. Shape dough into a roll, wrap in plastic wrap, and chill at least 1 hour.
5. Preheat oven to 375 degrees.
6. Roll dough 1/8 inch thick on lightly floured surface. Cut into Santa shapes (or other shapes if you so desire). For filled cookies, roll the dough out slightly thinner and put cookies together in pairs with 1 teaspoon of your favorite filling or jam. Press edges together with tines of fork. Then bake.
7. Place on ungreased cookie sheet. Bake 8-10 minutes or until light brown.
8. After the cookies cool, decorate them as you both desire.

Makes about 10-12 dozen. Wrapped dough will store 1 to 2 weeks in refrigerator.

SANTA'S ORANGE FROTH

Along with Santa's cookies leave a glass full of this yummy drink.

Whip in blender: 3 cups water, 6 ounces frozen orange juice concentrate, 1 cup powdered milk, and 1 tablespoon coconut. Pour into glass and sprinkle a dash of nutmeg on the top.

Remember to leave a carrot for Rudolph, too!

ACTIVITIES

SANTA'S COOKIE PLATE

Santa will be honored to have his snack served on this personalized plate.

1. Trace your child's hands (fingers closed in a mitten style) on construction paper. Help her cut them out, and give her what help she needs with steps 2-6.

2. Cut out two eyes, a nose, a wide-smiling mouth, and a triangular Santa hat from construction paper.

3. Glue eyes, nose, and mouth onto a white paper plate.

4. Staple hat onto top of Santa's head. Staple hands so they overlap each other over Santa's mouth.

5. Glue cotton balls on hat tip and hat brim, and for Santa's hair and beard.

6. Write on the top hand, OPEN. On the inside of each hand write questions your child wants to ask Santa or a note to Santa, and have her sign her name.

7. Santa's cookie can be placed on the mouth and then covered by the hands as a surprise for him to find.

Won't your child be thrilled to read Santa's answers to her questions on Christmas morning?

SANTA'S BAG GAME

Everyone loves Santa; everyone loves to pretend to be Santa. Role-play being Santa with this easy guessing game.

1. Get a pillowcase.

2. Take turns pretending to be Santa and collect objects to put in your bag to deliver for Christmas. Swing the bag over your back, and when you arrive at your destination, have your child guess what the items might be inside your Santa bag. You may wish to collect all toys, or all Christmas things, or all things that start with a certain letter. Try this game in a variety of ways.

CHRISTMAS DECORATIONS RIDE

By tonight all the people who decorate their homes and yards for Christmas will have finished. Plan a few extra minutes to go for a drive around town to see the beauty. When you come home have your child draw his favorite scene. You may wish to use a paper punch to cut out holes from colored construction paper to symbolize the Christmas lights.

FIFTH WEEK

Goodbye Old, Hello New

When we think about New Year's Eve, visions of confetti, party hats, horns, blowers, streamers, balloons, and merriment come to mind. Most people party that evening to say goodbye to the outgoing year and to welcome the new year. It traditionally is not considered a holiday that children celebrate. Staying up until midnight doesn't make much sense for young ones. But why must the celebration take place at midnight? Perhaps it can be celebrated on New Year's Day at breakfast or lunchtime. Below are some suggestions for ways to bring in the new year with your child at whatever time is most appropriate for your family schedule.

READINGS

Goodbye Old Year, Hello New Year by Frank Modell (Greenwillow Books)

Two good friends and neighbors, Marvin and Milton, make plans to have their own New Year's Eve celebration. Since they are too young to stay awake until midnight, they decide to set their alarm clocks to wake them for their midnight festivities . . . but they sleep right through the alarm! They do, however, find their own ways to celebrate.

Little Bear's New Year's Party by Janice Brustlein (Lothrop, Lee & Shepard Co.)

Little Bear has never been invited to a New Year's Eve party, but rather than being sad about it, he plans a party of his own.

Happy New Year by Emily Kelley (Carolrhoda Books)

Different countries have different ways to celebrate the new year. This book presents seven other nations' customs and festivities. Readers will enjoy learning the traditions of others and may want to add some of these ideas to their own New Year's celebration.

RECITINGS

WHERE, OH WHERE HAS 1990 GONE?
(Sung to "Where, Oh Where Has My Little Dog Gone?")

Oh, where, oh where has 1990 gone?
Oh, where, oh where can it be?
With its good days and bad
And the fun that we had,
Oh where, oh where can it be?

I spent 3650 hours asleep in bed.
And 1095 hours eating food.
With 1825 hours at play and 1095 hours in school,
I think it was all pretty good!

Calculate an approximate average of hours that suits your child, if you'd like, and change the numbers in the last verse. You will also have to change "1990" to the appropriate year.

HAPPY NEW YEAR'S TO YOU
(Sung to "Happy Birthday to You")

Happy New Year's to you,
Happy New Year's to you.
I hope that this new year
Will be a good one for you.

Happy New Year's to you,
Happy New Year's to you.
Just think what might happen
In this year for you.

A tooth you might lose,
New friends you might choose,
So many surprises . . .
So Happy New Year's to you.

RECIPES

WASSAIL BOWL

The tradition of drinking from the wassail bowl originated in Old England when families would drink this hot spicy drink on New Year's Day. A ring would be dropped into the bowl and the person who got the ring in his cup would supposedly get married that year. (You may want to change this tradition a bit and reward the "ring-bearer" in a more appropriate manner!)

1. Mix in a large pot: 1 cup apple juice, ⅙ cup lemon juice, 1 cup cranberry juice, ⅛ cup sugar, 1 cup herbal tea (any flavor), 1 stick cinnamon, ½ cup orange juice, 3 whole cloves.
2. Simmer for 30 minutes.
3. Remove cinnamon sticks and cloves. Serve warm. Serves 5.

NEW YEAR FRUIT SALAD

You may wish to use the grapes as part of a fruit salad that you can serve with the pancakes. Welcome in the new year with at least one new kind of fruit in your salad. Perhaps you can add kiwi, pomegranate, Asian pear, kumquats, or any other fruit your child has not yet tried. Add coconut, sunflower seeds, dried fruit, or chopped nuts.

CHILDREN'S NEW YEAR'S CELEBRATION

Gather together some noisemakers—whether traditional party favor types or pots and pans with spoons; play drums; kazoos—whatever you have in the house that is appropriate.

Make some confetti-stuffed balloons (see activities below).

On your designated New Year's Eve have everyone gather together and begin your countdown: "10, 9, 8, 7, 6, 5, 4, 3, 2, 1 . . . Happy New Year!" Let the festivities begin! Pop the balloons, shake your noise-makers. Have someone say the family toast (see activities below) as you all sip on wassail.

Serve pancakes with your wassail bowl. The French people eat them on New Year's Day to bring them good luck for the rest of the year. (See Chapter Six for the Home-made Pancake recipe and other pancake ideas.)

Also have 12 grapes for each person. According to a Spanish tradition, when the clock strikes 12 on New Year's Eve everyone eats 12 grapes, each one signifying good luck for each month of the coming year. Enjoy the rest of your food and, of course, each other.

ACTIVITIES

CONFETTI-STUFFED BALLOONS

Using a paper punch, punch holes out of pieces of various colors of construction paper. Stuff the pieces of confetti into deflated balloons, then blow the balloons up. Your child might enjoy doing some of this with you.

NEW YEAR'S TOAST

Make up a special toast that will be meaningful for your family. Work on it together as a kind of family project. Include wishes and hopes for the new year that will be important for your whole family.

SUPERLATIVES

When all the excitement dies down, reflect on the past year and fill out superlatives like the ones suggested below:

- best days of the year
- farthest traveled in the year
- worst days of the year
- biggest excitement of the year
- favorite book read in the year
- favorite foods of the year
- favorite TV program of the year
- favorite songs of the year
- most fun in the year

What were your child's favorite things from this past year? What were yours? Did your answers tend to center around times shared with each other?

Children are our most precious possessions, and being there to share a story or an activity will build and strengthen your relationship. Make it your New Year's resolution now to continue taking time out together in the years to come!

INDEX

INDEX